Tomorrow's
Sights and Sounds

A REPOSITORY OF DREAMS
Chronicle of Language

SHORT STORIES
WORDS
POEMS
DEVOTIONS
LESSONS

ALBERT F. SCHMID

WESTBOW
PRESS®
A DIVISION OF THOMAS NELSON
& ZONDERVAN

Scripture taken from the Holy Bible, NEW INTERNATIONAL VERSION®. Copyright © 1973, 1978, 1984 by Biblica, Inc. All rights reserved worldwide. Used by permission. NEW INTERNATIONAL VERSION® and NIV® are registered trademarks of Biblica, Inc. Use of either trademark for the offering of goods or services requires the prior written consent of Biblica US, Inc.

WestBow Press books may be ordered through booksellers or by contacting:

WestBow Press
A Division of Thomas Nelson & Zondervan
1663 Liberty Drive
Bloomington, IN 47403
www.westbowpress.com
1 (866) 928-1240

Because of the dynamic nature of the Internet, any web addresses or links contained in this book may have changed since publication and may no longer be valid. The views expressed in this work are solely those of the author and do not necessarily reflect the views of the publisher, and the publisher hereby disclaims any responsibility for them.

Any people depicted in stock imagery provided by Thinkstock are models, and such images are being used for illustrative purposes only. Certain stock imagery © Thinkstock.

ISBN: 978-1-5127-0937-7 (sc)
ISBN: 978-1-5127-0938-4 (hc)
ISBN: 978-1-5127-0936-0 (e)

Library of Congress Control Number: 2015913576

Print information available on the last page.

WestBow Press rev. date: 10/02/2015

CONTENTS

BLESSINGS

A blessing cannot be kept. If it is stopped with the recipient, then the blessing disappears.

We are blessed significantly in many ways, but particularly by being a member of the First Baptist Church of East Greenwich. The church provides us the opportunity to minister and evangelize while serving on the Visitation Committee and other church related missions.

We are the recipients of a blessing and we need to keep that blessing working by being the source of the blessing to other people.

Rev. Albert F. Schmid
September 29, 2015

PREFACE

Dedications and Disclaimers

Writing a book is like looking into a mirror and transforming the image to the written word. Someone once said that a picture is worth a thousand words. The biblical writer, David proclaims, **"Your word... a light for my path."** Psalm 105 NIV. In order to see and understand the word we must have Light and that light comes from the Lord.

Very little is needed to make a happy life. It merely depends on yourself, All that is within you, in your way of thinking and your relationship with God. I consider myself blessed because I have been given the opportunity to live a Happy life.

It is wonderful to be able to look back upon my past with reflection to share Some of the memories and stories of which I write. I appreciate the encouragement and support that has come from The First Baptist Churches in Wickford And East Greenwich, Rhode Island.

My wife Audrey continues to be my number one critic and guide and provides the support and encouragement that is so important.

Coming together is a beginning;
Keeping together is progress;
Working together is success.

Henry Ford

COLORS ARE THE SMILES OF NATURE

Books challenge the reader to generate a definition of a Word. For example, the word **colors** may be used to describe the nature or the feelings of a wonderful book or the gift of the author for writing.

Colors may be bright, they may blend with their surroundings. They may be spectacular and pleasing to the eye. They may convey a special meaning or share a particular story. Colors can be diverse and are often very distinctive. Colors have a message without saying anything more.

When my children were small I would ask them, "What are the colors of a traffic light and what do they mean?" They would answer:

RED means STOP.
GREEN means GO
YELLOW means LET YOUR FRIEND GO FIRST.

Even BLACK has an element of intrigue and suspense. Writing lets your colors shine through and helps to paint the picture of intent. God bless us always in the use of colorful words.

THE CHRONICLE OF LANGUAGE

There is a widely accepted theory that the very first structured human verbal language emerged roughly 150,000 years ago in East Africa. From grunts and groans, signs and symbols man developed a way to communicate with one another. The sound, which became known as a word, was much more easily used than hieroglyphics or pictures. As the use of words grew a language emerged and as humans spread around the world more than 6,000 major languages and thousands of different dialects developed. Other experts tell us that the genesis was only 35,000 years ago. But, on the other hand we are discovering today, in the 21st Century, tribes of Indians living in the upper Amazon River who communicate with a totally different language and strange dialects.

As the world becomes smaller, by modern technology and instant communications, many of these languages are gradually losing their individuality and are being merged into a common use. At the same time we find that even in our own society a new language developing through the use of iPods' and cell phones that have produced a new hybrid called **texting.** Words change their form, to speed up communications. New words are created that mean different things. In some cases they may even be considered a "coded Message."

Some experts predict that with a gradual change over the next couple of centuries the world will return to a single tongue. We will have to wait and see.

It was about 3500 B. C. that some bright individual decided it was time to record the words of his language. It started with some mechanical device like a pointed stick, he pressed some symbols he had invented into mud, clay or on papyrus. He found he could even use fabric or soft stone. He learned that he could make words that described events and recorded history. An example is, 1 Chronicles and 2nd Chronicles found in the Old Testament of the Bible. The two books deal mainly with the chronology and genecology of the Jewish people.

But, the idea of using words placed on paper or stone caught on quickly and soon many of the language talkers became language writers. Each language generated its own rules and symbols. The process was complicated, so that only about 200 of the languages ever became written and fewer were widely printed and/or published. The Bible was recorded using mainly the Latin, Greek and Hebrew languages.

Boiled down, the basic unit of any language is the **word.** And on that note we begin this Copia verborum.

DEVOTIONALS. The way God works in our everyday life humble Truth is told and the reader can identify with His graciousness. He reveal His love and care of us through HIS mercy. All that He does for us.

WORDS-POEMS-YARNS -
PARABLES - DEVOTIONALS

The WORD apportionment is devoted to how words are used, what is the standard, is it universally understood and what misused words really accomplish.

POEMS are nothing more than a bunch of words arranged in rhyme or blank verse that convey a certain truth or emotion. The book of Psalms in the Old Testament is a collection of poems, and hymns and lessons written by David, Israel's most celebrated King. Psalms were written for solitary singing or meditation. Some Psalms were sung by soldiers while marching to battle. Psalms were collected as guides to worship, prayer and teaching of God.

YARNS. A Yankee way of using a story or tale make a point. Abandon the line structure of poems and create any arrangement of words to enthrall the reader. Use an element of humor in writing a Yarn.

PARABLES. Jesus' favorite method of teaching was to tell a story that the listener could identify and relate to. The method was to compare the story to God's word as a lesson. A favorite definition of parable is, **"An earthly story with a heavenly meaning."**

DEVOTIONALS. The use of words, poems, yarns and parables to tell of God's love and faith in the children He has created. His special gift to all mankind for eternal life through His son Jesus Christ.

Words are Tomorrow's Sights and Sounds.

WORDS

Body language, music, and even types of noise are means of communication, but words still remain our primary method for transfer of thought. Someday we may be able to exchange information from the brain to another person directly. But for now, we are generally restricted to the fragile and imprecise medium of words.

The basic problem with words is that they mean different things to different people. Long, polysyllabic words which require reference to a dictionary are generally subject to mutual misunderstanding. Small, frequently used words often fail to have effective thought transfer. This seems particularly true of words that describe some of the most fundamental concepts of our lives and relationships.

In trying to define exactly what these basic words mean, I found no easy task, but as an attempt I want to present the following words to challenge the reader to generate their own definitions so that we will understand what they mean when they are used.

FAITH	BELIEF
HOPE	DUTY
LOVE	HONOR
CHARITY	COURAGE
TRUTH	COMMITMENT

FAITH

Belief is structured, has a foundation, is supportable and differs from faith. **Faith** is much wider, it is inclusive, open without form. It is mystical and cannot be quantified. Yet, over the course of history it has motivated much good and has driven mankind to accomplish many of the world's greatest works.

Faith has sponsored and has generated some of the world's greatest structures. It has changed the geography, modified the borders and made the world seem smaller. It has changed the course of rivers and altered the environment. Faith has turned the land from dry, nonproductive areas to moist high prolific farm lands. Faith has reorganized t. the minds and morays of every civilization.

Faith has no chemical, physical, psychological, or mental potential. Therefore, Faith finds itself centered on one of three foci:

1. on a deity outside of the tangible into the spiritual realm. Confirmed by the Biblical quotation: *"Now faith is being sure of what we hope and certain of What we cannot see." Hebrews 11:1.*

2. on a person, very real, physical, a leader. A teacher, a supervisor, a coach, an elected representative, an official, a military leader, a diplomat, who has the Ability to hold things together and encourages his followers to cope successfully in the most difficult circumstances, even seemingly accomplishing the impossible.

3. A program, philosophy or cause. Faith transcends the persona of the one who moves to embrace the movement itself, like the Crusades to the Holy Land, Apostle Paul's three missionary journeys and his final trip to Rome, even the modern day Civil Rights marches? Faith that convinces the follower of the righteousness of the cause and the firm belief that it will eventually have A successful outcome.

The willingness to dedicate oneself may come from outside influences and controls. Or more mystically and powerfully persistent from that which seems to be inside revelations. And so we return to the opening statement and the very mystic nature of this wonderful phenomenon, Faith.

"The substance of things hoped for, the evidence of things not seen." Heb. 11: 1

HOPE

If Faith can be anchored and firm we find **Hope** is insecure, fragile and vaporous. It is just the expression of what we would like things to be. It has no foundation in reality or substance. It is like hanging onto a thought or aspiration with cliff edge hardened fingernails.

Hope cannot be analyzed or synthesized. An engineer dismisses it as irrational. The scientist thinks it is nice but impractical. A mathematician says it doesn't add up. And yet, without Hope there is precious little vision for the future. Without the optimism of Hope life gets bogged down in the mire of mud of boring practicality. Without Hope disaster brings only death, the mediocre retains status quo and the dark valley never sees the sun.

It is in the Euclidian absurdity of **Hope** that the dammed find reason to struggle and overcome. Hope admits the utter ridiculousness of its position and then goes on to undergird and support its eventual realization. Hope is what holds life together when all the glue of security has dissolved.

**"Love protects, always trusts, always hopes,
and always perseveres." 1 Cor. 13:**

LOVE

Love is probably the most misused word in the English language. It is used to describe the "Noble passion" -- and the affection felt for a specific brand of toilet issue. "Love your hair," Love that soup," "Love that song," "That is a lovely tie." We love our homes, we love our cars, we love those drinks" --- ad infinitum. How we torture the meaning of that wonderful word. Greeks had the answer. They have three words for **Love: Eros, Phileo, and Agape.**

Eros

Without this love it is doubtful that any of us would be here today. This is the love which supports the continuation of the species by the bringing together the male and female to create the next generation. It is a way that humankind attempts to assure its immortality. Eros Love has had a vast impact on history.

Procreation is a byproduct of Eros Love. One has to wonder if Eros is limited to man and if it extends to other species, animals, birds, or fish. We do know that some species have Eros that produces a mating for life. The Canada goose and the Cardinal are two birds who practice a monogamous relationship. The Seal and the Penguin and other mammals do likewise. This is evidence of a case of Eros love. It is essentially a very selfish love with very specific objectives. It is from Eros, of course, that we derive the word Erotic, with all of its overtone.

Phileo

Phileo love has completely different emotion. Phileo is brotherly and/or sisterly love. No sexual implications involved. This becomes family affection at its best. It is the thing that makes for sacrifice, the protection of a buddy in a foxhole, the ultimate sacrifice to save a friend. This love is not completely unselfish. It anticipates a certain reciprocity, a return of the emotion, a two way street for the implied mutual support.

Agape

Agape love is the true unselfish love. It is the sacrifice and support for the unknown recipient, expecting and receiving no compensation or recognition. The cynic may say, but what about the warm inner feeling generated by a gift to the victims of a Tsunami, or earthquake on the other side of the world. These clouds can be ethically rationalized and erased but they aren't the only gifts that are received by the needy. The act is agape and its impulse is essentially pure. Put them all together, they are the streams of emotion that make us human, the lack of which reverts us to the bottom of the animal world. *"And now these three remain: faith, hope and love, but the greatest of these is love."* **1 Cor. 13: 13**

CHARITY

An old adage says "Charity begins at home." Elbert Hubbard defined Charity as, "The thing that begins at home and usually stays there." Many people believe that giving creates a deductible that affects their tax liability. Why folks give, to whom they give, and the amount of the gift is a personal matter. Experts in Giving USA believe that tax considerations are not necessarily the determining factor. The truth is the mission or the work of the organization and a personal solicitation by someone they know are the primary reasons that people give. A conservative estimate of giving to charities in the USA is over 200 billion dollars a year.

Pledge programs, fund raising campaigns, specific fund drives and other methods are used to raise money. Often the campaign offers a way for the giver to gain recognition. Your name on a plaque, recognition in a corporate program. A name on a sign, the receiving of special membership incentives, and more. There are many ways to gain an advantage of temporary immortality.

The important thing is the use of the funds generated. How much of the monies are siphoned off for administrative costs or additional promotions. Religious institutions and churches are the recipients of more than 47% of the gifts contributed by Americans. The Mormon Church and other conservative denomination regard a tithe of 10% right off the top to be their obligation. They believe that their giving begins after the tithe is made. Other groups are less economically dedicated.

Many people give because it supports their egos, makes them feel good. In one church a man gave generously to the church by carefully laying a new $100 bill in the collection plate so that everyone who saw it would think that he was very righteous. Then there are others who give without fanfare and do not seek recognition. Their gift is the act of returning to the Lord a portion of that they have received from Him. It is done subtly and often anonymously.

The Europeans having state supported churches, welfare programs, support for the sick and aged, care for the poor, national educational institutions and more, can't understand why we in America ante up more than 200 billion dollars a year voluntarily. Shouldn't the state take care of all of that and be taxed accordingly? Perhaps it has something to do with freedom!

The perfection and ornament of religion.

TRUTH

Someone said, that Truth is a "Reassuring breeze wafting across the swamp of duplicity through the forest of misrepresentation and transiting the desert of half the story." It reaches us to be received with acceptance, understanding and belief.

In the hands of the priest, the sage, the missionary, the religious crusader, truth is a compendium of nostrums, formulated to support a specific stand or objective. Truth is a weapon in the hands of the unscrupulous when used to achieve personal gains by weakening the objective through rubbing its salt into open wounds. Herbert Read said, "It is what men kill each other for."

Raw truth, mechanically promulgated without regard to effect can result in the exact opposite of its intent to stabilize society. Truth is the secret of eloquence and of virtue and the basis of moral authority. It is the highest summit of art and life."

What then is the Truth?

BELIEF

In spite of what some might think, everyone has a belief in something. Even the staunchest agnostic or atheist strongly supports his belief.

All cultures from the beginning of time have strived to find and establish an identity with some force outside of themselves in which they could believe. A belief in which they could find hope of receiving something back. One that they could pay homage to. The primitive people worshipped natural phenomena. They worshipped fire, wind, heavenly bodies, the sea and the mountains. The Romans and Greeks made up their special gods; god of the hunt, god of love, god of war. The Greeks were so concerned that they might miss one they even made a statue to the Unknown God.

Three of the largest religious groups are the Jewish, Muslim and Christian believers. All have a common origins and a belief in a monotheistic god. It started with a prosperous herdsman and his family who lived in one of the world's most fertile areas, near the Chaldeans. They lived in an extended valley formed by two rivers, the Tigris and the Euphrates. The herdsman, Terah, took his son Abram and his grandson Lot and moved his family and their herds to Canaan. It was a long journey and the trip was hazardous and difficult. Something happened and they stopped in Haran, which was about half way to Canaan. It was here that Terah died.

Now, the history of this fledgling tribe and their relationship with its very personal single God they called Jehovah, began. God directed Abram to begin the journey to Canaan again. God promised

Abram (later called Abraham) many things: The possession of land; the blessings of a tremendous progeny; great success. This puzzled Abram since the land that God promised was already populated and Abram's wife could not bear children it was obvious that Abram would have no heirs. It was also strange because the land promised was in no way as productive as the one they had left. During Abraham's life the people experienced great famines and the tribe had to move to Egypt for food several times in order to survive.

But Abraham believed and he directed his people to follow God. However, when the Hebrews followed God's directions and commands they prospered, when they disobeyed they suffered grievously. Amazingly, they always seemed to be given another chance. They were God's chosen people.

During the journey to Canaan the family split and one son moved on to become the leader of an off shoot tribe which emerged as the ancestors of the Muslims. With a different interpretation they believed in a single deity now called Allah. Still one god.

The story of the Hebrews, later called Jews, has been one of continual problems and relentless persecution. The thing that held them together through the most terrible experiences has been their firm belief in God. The belief that they are a very unique and special people who have been given a promise from their Lord, Jehovah.

Two thousand years ago a New Hebrew leader arose. Jesus of Nazareth. Born of a virgin, in the most humble conditions Jesus became a very charismatic teacher who preached against the bureaucracy of the religious leaders of his day. His doctrine was simple basic love and care.

Jesus' outstanding success in reaching the oppressed and the down trodden put him at odds with the religious and the temporal leaders to the point that they decided to publicly execute him. The most horrendous and shameful death witnessed by the people was by crucifixion. Jesus was crucified at Golgotha along with two other criminals. This should have stopped the movement and we would never have known Christianity.

But, Jesus' followers believed him and knew that he was the son of God. They witnessed his death and his resurrection as had been prophesied in the Old Testament. They passionately began to follow his teaching, went forth to furthest corner of the known world to spread the gospel of the risen Savior and God's promise of eternal life through His son Jesus Christ.

Considering the history and spread of Christianity from such an inconsequential start to the scope and influence it has had over twenty centuries and continues to have today, it is impossible to pass it off as just another cult. This must be the verity in which I believe.

It is the strongest argument.

DUTY

Duty is the action which causes better to exist in the universe than any possible alternative. It is the act of an individual who knows something should be done and is bound to do it, or perform specific projects which are designed to help other people or mankind in general.

Duty may be divided into two concepts; individual **and contractual.**

Individual duty is that which is taken upon oneself voluntarily -- without any legal pressure but only from a feeling of personal obligation. An example: An individual believes that it is his duty to provide social and financial support to his aging parents. His rational is that is it time to repay them for giving him life and nurture in his growing years. Unlike the legal demands to provide child support, there is no such requirement to provide parent support. It is a personal matter, a duty self-imported.

Contractual duty is that which is assumed by an individual because of his association with an organization, cause or belief. When one raises their right hand and takes an oath of office or joins the military, a fraternal organization, the Boy or Girl Scouts, they automatically assume the duties and accept the regulations of that service. There are no options and little opportunity not to follow the duties of the service. Even in peace time one has the option of joining or not joining, but once the commitment is made the structure of the organization prevails. It is your duty to comply and follow the rules. It is the glue that holds the group together.

So why should a person assume the responsibilities and duties, individual or contractual, and the demands and tough obligations derived from them? Often it is because the person has the inner strength and maturity to cause him to recognize the complete and responsible nature he inherits from the society in which he lives. Sometimes it is done through the encouragement received from a parent, a grandparent or from a mentor.

Often a belief or an idea develops by assuming that certain duties, particularly those of a contractual nature, will make you a better person. The lack of assumption of duty and obligation of some kind gives evidence of immaturity, or a weak and spineless individual, entirely selfish and self-centered.

The steel of Duty makes the individual a real person!

HONOR

The word **Honor** has multiple meanings. It may be used as a verb, a noun or an adjective.

Early use of the word honor as a verb, is found in the English translation of the 5th Commandment. "Honor your father and your mother that you may live long in the land that the Lord your God is giving to you." (Ex 20: 12 NIV) This is the only commandment with a promised happy reward. The demand does not require that we love or even respect our parents, merely honor or recognize them as our parents. Recognition is the key word. If it were not for them we wouldn't exist. Recognition and honor implies it is our duty to them who gave us birth.

The verb honor is used to describe other kinds of recognition. Recognition for achievement in sports, in business in academics and even in longevity. An entire industry deals with plaques, medals, trophies, scrolls, certificates and even banquets for the purpose of honoring individuals, groups and achievers.

Used as a noun we find judges and justices are addressed as "Your Honor", whether they truly represent that quality might be questioned. However, Honor at its truest sense is a personal quality that is at the heart of the individual. We swear or affirm, "On My Honor". The Boy Scouts of American begin their Oath with, "On my honor I will do my best to do my duty to God and my country. To help other people at all times, to keep myself physically strong, mentality awake and morally straight."

Honor is the cleanest, most sacred, purest of qualifies. It is completely devoid of self-aggrandizement, dedicated to the best in society, a personal quality to be protected by the individual at any cost from any form of impingement or stain.

**"Honor is the moral conscience of the
great." William D'Avenant**

COURAGE

Courage, rightly esteemed, is the first of human qualities. It is the quality that guarantees all others. The Apostle Paul writing to the church at Corinth says, ***"Be on your guard; stand firm in the faith; be men of courage; be strong. Do everything in love." 1 Corinthians 16: 13-14.***

The Oxford Dictionary defines the noun "courage "as the ability to disregard fear.' This can be expressed in a multitude of different ways; including, but not limited to taking your very first step as a toddler; riding off on a two wheel bike without the training wheels, or making your first landing aboard an aircraft carrier. Socrates says courage is, "Knowing what not to fear."

Courage is also expressed as an act of bravery, chivalry, and intrepidness. General W. T. Sherman said, "Courage is a perfect sensibility of the measure of danger and a mental willingness to endure it.

Other synonyms might include: dauntlessness, fortitude, tenacity, or resolution. Ernest Hemingway said, "Courage is grace under pressure."

I challenge you to have the courage to read this book, Tomorrow's Sights and Sounds.

COMMITMENT

The word commitment is a strong and lasting word. Regarded as a positive, it can mean a pledge, a responsibility an agreement, an act of pulling together. Using commitment in a negative sense would imply incarceration, or an obligation that restricts freedom of action. Let's consider the positive meaning.

Making a commitment can be defined as the process of engaging in or entering into an obligation that pledges or encumbers oneself to a moral course or policy. A pledge to your church's financial budget is a commitment.

In the scriptures David speaks to God: *"My times are in your hands, deliver me from my enemies and those who purse me." Psalm 30: 15.* David is talking about his day to day circumstances and in this manner, he was confirming that he was committing his spirit to the Lord and trusting his life to God. David was making a commitment.

Understanding the meaning of making a commitment, we trust that you will be committed to reading this epistle.

We have only sampled a few words of the English language. Of the 10 words that were chosen, one could agree that they all appear somewhere in the scriptures. They are a foundation to many oaths, pledges, and declarations. An example is the Boy Scouts of America Oath and Promise:

"On my honor I will do my best,
To do my duty to God and my country
To help other people at all times.
To keep myself physically strong,
Mentality alert, and morally straight."
A scout is: Trustworthy
Loyal
Helpful
Friendly
Courteous
Kind
Obedient
Cheerful
Thrifty
Brave
Clean, and
Reverent

We have only scratched the surface of English words. The Oxford Dictionary has more than 20 volumes of words, not including many foreign words that have found their way into the English through the development of 21st century technology, medicine, computer science, space travel, and many other sources. A conservative estimate of the number of words exceeds one million two hundred eighty thousand. (1,280,000)

I trust that you have been challenged to read on and search TOMORROW'S **SIGHTS and SOUNDS** for words and stories both old and new.

POEMS, A BEAUTIFUL SOUND IN ANY LANGUAGE

THE HISTORY OF POETRY

Poetry may predate literacy. The earliest poetry is thought to have been recited or sung, employing different ways of remembering events of, history, genealogy and law. Poetry is often closely related to traditions. The earliest poetry existed in the form of hymns or chants. Many poems surviving through history are recorded prayers or stories about religious subject matter. They also include historical accounts, admonitions, and instructions for everyday activities, love songs and fiction. The use of repeated phases are building blocks in larger poetic units. A rhythmic and repetitious form makes a long story easier to remember, to retell, memorize or transmit orally.

One commercial application of poetry, that is classic, is the Burma Shave signs, that date from the early twenties through 2005. They are signs with poetic slogans that line the roads of America from coast to coast advertising a shaving cream. An example would be:

> To Change that shaving job to joy
> You got to use the real McCoy.
> *Burma Shave*

> Or: Why is it when you try to pass
> The guy in front goes twice as fast?
> *Burma Shave*

Years ago my family lived in Connecticut and as the children grew up we would take frequent trips around New England to visit the historical sights, see the scenery and learn as much as we could about our country. Driving along rural area roads we would often see a series of *Burma Shave* signs that always made the trip more enjoyable. The children would play games to see who could spot and read the sign first. This is one example of using poetry in advertising. I remember many of the signs but I must admit that I have never purchased a tube of *Burma Shave*. Maybe it is about time. To this day I wonder why the jingles were so popular. Perhaps it is because they contain an element of humor or a word of caution in them.

The largest book in the Old Testament is Psalms. With 150 chapters, it is a book of poetry, not doctrinal essays. David, the most celebrated King of Israel, is connected to 73 of the Psalms either as the writer or recipient. Other writers include Asaph, Solomon and Moses. Psalms may be considered as entries in a diary – they reflect people's most intimate encounters with God. When reading Psalms one must read with your heart as well as your mind. Poetry is lasting evidence when connected to a memory or an incident.

RULES FOR LIVING

We are nearly over-whelmed with rules, edicts, commandments and customs for righteous living. The question is, what works for you? Perhaps the following suggestions may help you to improve your life style.

1. Know Thyself
2. Play Tough
3. Try, Try Again
4. Remain Curious
5. Honor your Commitments
6. Count your Blessings
7. Be mindful of others.
8. Think and Act with Passion.

Know Thyself

Many never really know who they are. They go through life always questioning their being, their talents and their future. Strive to know who you are and focus on your objectives and your interests.

Play Tough

People sometimes think that life is a "cake walk." Others only complain that life is difficult and unyielding. The axiom: "When the times get tough, the tough get going," is a truism. Play tough. Play to win for maximum accomplishment.

Try, Try Again

Often our first attempt ends in failure. My football coach would always say when I got knocked down, "Get up husky and shake it off, try again." Go for it. Try again.

Remain Curious

Learn as much as you can about your profession or what you choose to be. Apply your knowledge and gain as much experience as possible. Curiosity promotes knowledge and knowledge will enable your success.

Honor Your Commitments

Know your limitations and do not exceed them. This applies to the physical, the mechanical and psychological limits. Keep your word, do what you said you would do and share your experiences with others.

Count Your Blessings

Be ever mindful of those around you; your family, your friends and your associates. Be thankful for the things that they share. And, above all, give thanks to the Lord for it is from Him we receive the blessings and unlimited love. Do not forget to praise Him for being your Lord. Thank Him for His compassion, his faith, His watch-care and safety.

Be mindful of others

Remember the Golden Rule, *"Do unto others as you would have them do unto you."* Be slow to anger but quick to praise. Forgiveness requires us to surrender our right to get even.

Think and Act with Passion

We are God's chosen people. We are to clothe ourselves with compassion, kindness, humility, gentleness and patience. Let the peace of Christ rule in your heart.

EVERLASTING POETRY

More than fifty years ago, when my five children were all young, and going to elementary school or kindergarten, we learned a poem that has stayed with us for all these years. The poem was entitled, TAFFY WAS A WELSHMAN.

At the time, we were raising registered collie puppies. The kennel was often filled to over-flowing with pups. The children shared in the feeding, grooming, cleaning of the pens, and training the little fellows. It was educational for the children to learn how to raise and take care of a pet. As the kids became more and more involved with the dogs we found a poem that fit and it was memorized by even the youngest who was in kindergarten. Taffy Was a Welshman.

The poem was memorable, and the children learned it quickly. Perhaps it was because the pups were all every active and full of the devil. The kids enjoyed naming each puppy and they quickly responded to their names. One beautiful little female was named Taffy. She had a full white collar, white paws, long collie nose with lovely sable and white markings. The name Taffy fit her well. The dogs all looked like Lassie, the famous dog in the movies.

The children loved her but she had her own personality. One could never anticipate what trouble she would get in or when it would happen. As a result, when this nursery rhyme was penned it stuck with Taffy. The story goes like this:

Taffy was a Welshman. Taffy was a thief.
Taffy came to my house, and stole a piece of beef.
I went to Taffy's house, Taffy was not home.
Taffy came to my house and stole a marrow bone.
I went to Taffy's house, Taffy was in bed.
I picked up the marrow bone and beat her on the head.

I have often wondered why the poem was so popular with the kids. Was it because the story was about their beloved dog? Was it because they identified with the prankishness of this lovable creature? Was it because of the rhythm of the poem? Was it the violence at the end? I may never know the answers to these question. And so it is with poetry; paint a picture; tell a story, make it rhyme; have it be easy to remembered; and end it with a moral. The rappers of the 21st century use these ways to popularize their messages today. **Everlasting life.**

THE NEED TO FLY

I watch as he turns to leave the hangar
His eyes scroll about as he takes it all in.
My heart feels the ties I know he is breaking,
I see a blink, then a tear as tries to grin.

Weather, flight plans, near and far away lands,
That's how he has lived this gentleman
This decision, put off for so long
Says, "Let's wrap it up," that is the plan.

The love for all he is, hits me so hard,
Watching his face like a living cue card.
The list of his losses he alone must review,
Will he allow me to help him get through?

Thousands of miles across the great sky,
Loving the privilege of his own wings to fly,
Seeing the world from a lofty view,
While modestly saying, "Well that's what I do."

A surprise in the offing is what we both need.
Time for the grandkids, and each other indeed.
Homebodies on outings by car or by air.
It won't matter to me as long as he's there.

Leisurely outings not controlled by a clock.
PA hand-hold stroll down some rustic dock.
Time to give back for all that has been,
Making room for each other away from life's din.

A prayer by Jabez was the very first glue.
Each was alone, but life is better by two.
This time in life may we spend it together?
This our own autumn, life's sweetest weather.

Thank God for the blessings on this . . . our love.

Audrey Schmid

PSALM 113

A hymn of praise to God

"Praise the Lord! Praise, O Servants of the Lord.
Praise the name of the Lord.
Let the name of the Lord be praised, both now and
Forever more.
From the rising of the sun to the place where it sets,
The name of the Lord is to be praised.
The Lord is exalted over all the nations. His glory
Above the heavens.
Who is like the Lord our God, the One who sits enthroned
On high, who stoops down to look on the
Heavens and earth?

He raises the poor from the dust and lifts the need from the
Ash heap; he seats them with princes, with the
Princes of their people.
He settles the barren woman in her home as a happy mother
Of children. Praise the Lord."

Psalm 113 NIV

WORLD CLASS

The world is like a looking-glass place,
That gives back to man the reflection of face.
A frown, a tear, a smile or a grin,
Will change the image of the place we are in.
Frown at the world and it soon will sour,
Laugh at the world and enjoy every hour.
The world can be measured with a line or a string,
But the world in our hearts will make us sing.

Al Schmid

ODE TO THE WINGS OF GOLD

A Naval Aviator's wings of gold,
When pinned on his chest with pride.
Will never come off, whether seen or not,
For they are there until he dies.

Those wings, though metal, are fused to the soul.
With adrenaline, adversity and froth.
No one can deny the feelings received,
When he successfully completes the loft.

In the world of flying, a life time of stories,
Of memories of ship-mates and friends.
Feelings last long after the flights are gone,
And the duty assignments have end.

When the flight suit is hung in the closet with care,
The Wings of Gold still exist.
A Naval Aviator's bearing speaks of what was,
But his heart clearly speaks of what is.

Go Navy!

Al Schmid
LCDR USNR

DEVOTIONALS, SHARING YOUR DREAMS

RHUBARB

the origin of the plant named Rhubarb comes from the Greek. Rah, which was the ancient name of the Volga River along whose banks the plant grew wild. The word barbarous was added resulting in the name Rhubarb. It is described as a plant having long green and red stalks that are edible when sweetened and cooked until tender. It is also called the pie plant. Where the suffix word barbarous came from is unknown except that although the stalks are edible the leaves contain oxalic acid and can be very toxic. The leaves are poisonous.

Rhubarb generally is eaten as a fruit, but botanically it is classified a vegetable. Because of the tartness rhubarb is usually combined with a considerable amount of sugar. It makes delicious rhubarb sauce, jam and pies. Thus the name pie plant. In America a traditional flavor combination is rhubarb and strawberries. **In England,** rhubarb is mixed with ginger. The plant has a high amount of Vitamin A.

Another definition of **rhubarb,** in an informal sense is: **a quarrel, fight, or heated discussion.** We do know that this usage was popularized in baseball. The Oxford English- Dictionary has the first citation in 1943. Mr. Red Barber, sports-announcer for the Brooklyn Dodgers baseball team, used the term rhubarb to describe an argument or a mix up on the field of play. The word may also have had a connection with **"hey rube"** used to describe a circus brawl or an incident in the theatre.

In any event, I love rhubarb pie. Make it strawberry-rhubarb and that is even better. Or I would even settle for some rhubarb sauce. I don't know if it is the tartness or the sweet taste but it is good. Very good!

When we moved from Illinois to Connecticut, my father-in law insisted that we take a bushel basket of rhubarb roots to plant at our new home. When we arrived in Connecticut I carefully planted them in the garden anticipating a bumper crop. But I had no success. I tried for several years and finally, on my last try, the plants took root and we had the most beautiful rhubarb plants I had ever seen. It provided me with several interesting object lessons we had beautiful rhubarb stalks growing next to our asparagus and tomato plants. I learned not to expect rhubarb to grow until the second year.

1. ***Rhubarb needs to go through a cold season in order to flourish.***
   As Christians we need to go through cold times and times of trial in Order to develop spiritually. In the scriptures we are consoled: Consider It pure joy, my brothers, whenever you face trials of many kinds, because You know that testing of your faith develops perseverance." James 1: 3 NIV

2. **Rhubarb leaves are poisonous and need to be cut away from the stalk.**
   As a follower of Jesus certain things have to be cut away from our lives. As we walk with Him. "Everyone who confesses the name of the Lord just turn away from wickedness." 2 Timothy 2: 19.

   For the best rhubarb desserts, you must add sugar or honey.
   When we accept Christ, the Holy Spirit enters our hearts and because of His sweet presence added to our lives, we are changed as we bear the fruit of the Spirit.

"The fruit of the spirit is love, joy, peace, patience, kindness, goodness, Faithfulness, gentleness and self-control. Against such things there is no law."

Galatians 5:22-25 (NIV)

Dear loving creator, sustain me, cleanse me, and change me. Amen

HAPPINESS AND FAITH

The chorus of the hymn, "At the Cross" ends with these cheerful words: ***"Now I am happy all the day."*** I don't know about you but I can't say that just because I know Jesus as my Savior that I am happy all the day. I believe that I am a rather optimistic person and I don't let things get me down often, but there are times when some circumstances don't warm my heart and make me smile. Like when my little Dachshund chews up his favorite stuffed toy trying to get the squeaker mechanism out. Ugh, cotton stuffing all over the place.

Troubles may make us wonder: Isn't our faith supposed to make us happy all the time? Shouldn't Jesus shelter us from disappointments, harm and danger? Isn't He like an umbrella that keeps us from getting wet whenever it rains? Some people teach these things but the Bible doesn't. God's word makes it clear that we **will** have troubles. Romans 8, for example, the epistle written by Paul, speaks frankly about tough times we could face. (Romans 8:35-39.) The fact is Jesus doesn't protect us from all trouble, but His love and companionship guide us as we go through it.

A more realistic attitude, other than being happy all the day, is to know that we are happier knowing Jesus and sharing His love than we were before we were saved. With Jesus Christ, we can have real joy and make it through even the bad times.

The hope we have in Jesus Christ
Brings joy into our hearts;
And when we know the love of God,
His peace He will impart.

Happiness depends on happenings, but Joy depends on Jesus.

David the writer of Psalms expresses his faith by saying to God, *"Your love is before my eyes, I walk guided by your faithfulness."* *Psalm 26: 3.*

In just a while the clouds will disappear. Once they do we will see a rainbow in the sky. Seems like now the world is colored grey, and is filled with nameless grief that seems to take our breath away. But eventuality the pain will leave and only joy will stay. We will breathe a sigh of relief and be able to smile again because nothing lasts forever in this world. God only sends the crosses we can bear and Jesus helps us to bear the burden of the cross.

NOT AS OLD AS I USED TO BE

The grocery store is a great place to get food for your body, but I discovered recently that it is a better place to find food for your heart, soul and mind. This happened the other day as I was walking through the store to pick up a quart of milk. You know how the dairy section is always located at the opposite end of the building, always in the back behind the bread, rolls and ice cream. Doesn't that make you wonder the effect of compulsive buying?

As I walked to the rear of the store I heard two ladies standing by the fruit and produce section, catching up on old times. The first one jokingly asked her friend how old she was and how she was getting along. The other lady answered very loudly so that everyone could hear, "Honey, I'm getting along fine and I am not nearly as old as I used to be." Everyone within ear shot laughed.

But, as I was leaving the checkout counter I realized that I am not nearly as old as I used to be either. I am not nearly as old as I used to be when I constantly worried about my bills and how I was going to pay them. Now I just trust in God and I always seemingly have enough.

I'm not as old as I used to be when I fretted about my weight and my thinning gray hair. Now I just look into the mirror and smile. The body looks a little older, but the soul on the inside is younger than ever.

I'm not as old as I used to be when I was always judging others, being angry with them, or worrying about what they thought of me.

Now I do my best to judge no one. I try to love everybody, and share my joy with the world. Life is too short to live any other way.

You don't have to be as old as you used to be either. God made all of us both ageless and forever young by choosing **love, joy and oneness with Him through His son Jesus Christ.** You can always keep growing younger and younger on the inside by sharing these truths with others. In sharing the love and joy that you receive you can give it to the world

By living from your soul you can stop counting your chronological age and counting birthdays and start living for eternity, because you will never again be as old as you used to be.

> Scripture: *"In the Lord's hands is the life*
> *of every creature and the breath*
> *Of all mankind. Does not the ear test*
> *words as the tongue tastes food?*
> *Is not wisdom found among the aged? Does not life*
> *bring understanding? To God belongs wisdom and*
> *power; counsel and understanding are his."*
> Job 12: 10-13

Sleep When the Rains Come

This year has been one of the wettest years in more than 100 years in the State of Rhode Island. Meteorologists and historians have agreed that the deluge of rain received in the spring and continuing through the summer months has been plentiful and can be considered unprecedented. The flood waters have come up fast and many families haven't had time to get out of their homes. One resident was heard to say, "I'm not leaving without my dog." Another home owner said. "It sounds like Niagara Falls in my basement."

Roads have turned into rivers, low level land have become lakes, bridges have been washed out and roads have become impassable. Even as the waters recede the roads have become rough and full of pot holes.

Basements that have always been dry ended up with water. If it happens again in another 100 years it will be too soon. With the results of our unusual weather system bringing a lot of rain I believe we may have a better appreciation for Noah and his Ark and the forty-days of rain that flooded the world. What we do know is God promised that He would never destroy the world with another flood. Some think that he is coming close again. Now that the sun is shining again and the waters are receding I am reminded of the story of the farmer and his hired hand who slept when the rains came.

A farmer owned land along a fertile valley and he needed a hired hand to help him with his work. He advertised for help but most the people were reluctant to work on the farm because of the risk of being flooded when the rainy season came. They dreaded the storms and the havoc on the buildings and destroying of the crops. As the farmer interviewed applicants for the job, he received a steady stream of refusals.

Finally, a short thin man, well past middle age, approached the farmer. "Are you a good farm hand?" asked the farmer. *"Well I sleep when the rains come," answered* the little man. Although puzzled by the answer, the farmer was desperate for help so he hired him. The little man worked well around the farm.

Busy from dawn to dusk. The farmer was satisfied with the man's work. He was pleased that he had hired this person.

Then one night the wind began to howl. Black rain clouds filled the sky. Lightning flashed in all quadrants. It began to rain and the rain turned to torrents. The farmer jumped out of bed, grabbed a light and rushed next door to the hired hand's sleeping quarters. He shook the little man and yelled, **"Get up! A storm is coming! We need to get things to higher ground!"** The little man rolled over in bed and said firmly, *"No sir. I told you that I sleep when the rains come."*

Enraged by the response the farmer was tempted to fire him on the spot. Instead, he hurried outside to prepare for the storm. He discovered that all of the farm equipment had been moved to higher ground. Sand bags had been filled and placed around the barn. The cows and chickens had been moved to a shelter above the flood plain. Everything possible had been done in preparation of the flood. The farmer then understood what his hired hand meant, so he returned to bed to sleep while the rains came.

When you are prepared spiritually, mentally and physically you have nothing to worry or fear.

The hired hand had secured the farm against the storm as best he could. We can secure ourselves against the storms of life by grounding ourselves in the **Word of God.** We don't need to understand, we just need to hold His hand in order to have peace in the middle of the storm.

Albert F. Schmid

The Bible says "I l*ift my eyes to the hills--from where will my help
come? My help comes from the Lord, the maker of heaven and
earth. He will not let your foot be moved -- He who watches over
Israel will neither slumber nor sleep. The Lord will keep you from
all harm, He will watch over your life. The Lord will watch over
you going out and coming in, from this time on and forevermore."*

Psalm. 121: 1-4, 7-8.

**Life is not about waiting for the storm to pass. It's
more about learning to sleep when it rains.**

WHAT IS ETERNAL VALUE

What things in this world have true eternal value? What is eternal? How do we define eternity? You may have heard someone say, "I have been waiting in this line for an eternity." No one knows how long eternity is. Webster defines eternity as *"Endless Time." The* Roy croft Dictionary says that eternity is the *"Sunday of Time."* and Lucretius says that eternity is, *"the sum of all sums."*

Life in this world is temporal, not eternal, and so the only part of life that has eternal value is that which lasts throughout eternity. Clearly, the most important value is having a relationship with Jesus Christ. Jesus the source of eternal life is the free gift that we receive from God for all who believe. *"For God so loved the **world that he gave his one and only son, that whoever believes in him shall not perish, but have eternal life." John 3:16.** Jesus said, **I am the way and the truth. No one comes to the Father except by me." John 14: 6***

Everyone is going to be somewhere, someday . . . for all eternity. Christians and non-Christians. The only difference is Christians have the promise of everlasting life while the rest, who have rejected Jesus, may expect everlasting punishment. Matthew 25: 46.

Are good works necessary for eternal life? Jesus did not teach that good deeds form the basis of our salvation. The Bible shows clearly that eternal life results from what God not what we do does. ... We are saved by God's grace not by our works. Still, God intends that those who receive His grace will also do good works. True faith is more than just claiming to have faith. Genuine love for God is expressed through service to others.

The material world offers us an abundance of things and the tendency is to seek after them. We all want to improve our way of life and desire to have our children have as much and even more than we do. Jesus taught us not to store up for ourselves earthly treasures that can be destroyed or stolen. (Matthew 6: 19-20.) After all, we brought nothing into this world, and we take nothing out of it.

Our core Christian values often get overlooked in our diligent quest for success and material comfort. In the midst of these earthly pursuits we often forget about God. There is certainly no eternal value in living our lives for ourselves, looking to get out of life all that we can, as society would have us to believe.

Yet there can be significant eternal value in what we do with our lives during the exceedingly short time we are here on earth. Scripture makes it clear that **good works** will not save us or keep us saved, it is equally clear that we will eternally be rewarded according to what we have done on earth. Christians are God's workers, in Christ Jesus, to do good works which God has prepared in advance for us to do. The good works pertain to serving the Lord the best way that we can with what He has given us with full dependence on Him.

The apostle Paul discusses the quality of the works that can bring eternal rewards. Comparing Christians to *builders* and the quality of our works with building materials, Paul informs us that the good materials that survive God's testing and have eternal value include *gold, silver, and costly stones.* Whereas, using inferior material of *wood, hay and straw* have no eternal value and will not be rewarded. (1 Corinthians 3: 11-13) In essence, Paul is telling us that not all of our conduct and works will merit rewards.

There are many ways our service to the Lord will bring us rewards. First, we need to recognize that every true believer has been set apart by God and for God. When we receive God's gift of salvation we were given certain spiritual gifts. If we think our gifts are insignificant we need to remember that Paul told the church in Corinth the body of Christ is made up of many parts. God has arranged the parts in the body just as He wanted them to be. Those parts of the body that seem weaker are indispensable. If you are exercising your spiritual gifts you are playing an important role in the body of Christ and doing that which has eternal value.

They humbly seek to edify the body and glorify God. Indeed, every little thing can add to the beautiful mosaic of what God can do when we each do our part. Spiritual gifts are God's way of administrating His grace to others.

When we have shown our love for God by obeying His commandments, when we persevere in the faith despite all opposition and affliction, when in His name we show mercy to the poor, the sick and the less fortunate, and when we help alleviate the pain and suffering that is all around us, then we *experience* eternal life.

HEAVENLY CROWNS

When I was growing up my mother used to say me, "You have earned another star in your crown," when I would do something especially good. I didn't realize the significance and the meaning until I began to study the scriptures and learned that there are five heavenly crowns mentioned in the New Testament.

The Greek word translated *"crown"* is stephanos (the source of the word is taken from Stephen the martyr) and means: "A badge of royalty, a prize in the public games, or a symbol of honor. It was generally used during the ancient Greek games and was represented by a wreath or garland of leaves placed on a victor's head as a reward for winning an athletic contest. A crown is also an emblem of sovereignty, worn by Kings and Queens depicting them as the leaders of their land. It was customary for a King to wear as many crowns as he had kingdoms.

The word *"crown"* is used figuratively in the New Testament telling of the rewards of Heaven that God promises those who are faithful. Paul's message to the church at Corinth describes how these crowns are awarded. *"Do you know that in a race all the runners run, but only one gets the prize? Run in such a way as to get the prize. Everyone who competes in the games goes into strict training. They do not get the crown that will last forever. Therefore I do not run like a man running aimlessly; I do not fight like a man beating the air. No, I beat my body and make it my slave so that after I have preached to others, I myself will not be disqualified for the prize."* 1 Corinthian 9: 24-27.

1) **Imperishable Crown.** Paul goes on and explains that many who run the race run it to receive the perishable crown, the garland of leaves but he calls it a temporal prize that soon turns brittle and falls apart. He reminds us that all things on earth are subject to decay and perish. Jesus urges us not to store our treasures on earth where moth and rust destroy and where thieves break in and steal but to run our race so as to receive the heavenly crown. Faithful endurance wins Heavenly rewards which is the inheritance of the **Imperishable Crown.**

2) **The Crown of Rejoicing.** Paul tells the Church at Philippi to rejoice always in the Lord, for all of the bountiful blessings that our gracious God has showered upon us. As Christians we have more in this life to rejoice about than anyone else. Luke tells us there is rejoicing even now in heaven. The crown of rejoicing will be our reward where God will wipe away every tear. There shall be no more death, nor sorrow, nor crying. There shall be no more pain, for the former things have passed away.

3) **The Crown of Righteousness.** In Timothy 4: 8 we learn the following: *"Finally, there is laid up for me the crown of righteousness, which the Lord, the righteous Judge, will give me on that Day, and not to me only but also to all who have loved His appearing."* We inherit this crown through the righteousness of Christ which is what gives us the right to it, and without which it cannot be obtained. Because it is obtained and possessed in a righteous way, and not by force and deceit as earthly crowns sometimes are. It is an everlasting crown promised to all who love the Lord and eagerly await his return. We know assuredly, that our reward is with Christ in eternity.

4) **The Crown of Glory.** In 1 Peter 5: 4 we read, *"And when the Chief Shepherd appears, you will receive the crown of glory that does not fade away."* The word glory is an interesting word referring to the very nature of God and His actions. It entails His great splendor and brightness. Remember Stephen

who, while being stoned to death, was able to look to the heavens and see the glory of God. The word glory also means the praise and honor that we give to God because of who He is. We as believers will be incredibly blessed to enter into the kingdom, in the very likeness of Christ Himself. Paul puts it this way, **"I consider that the sufferings of this present time are not worthy to be compared with the glory which shall be revealed to us in heaven."**

5) **The Crown of Life.** Revelation 2:10, gives us some great advice: *"Do not fear any of those things which you are about to suffer. Indeed the devil is about to throw some of you into prison, that you may be tested, and you will have tribulation ten days. Be faithful until death, and I will give you the crown of life."*

The crown is for all believers, but it is especially dear to those who endure sufferings, who bravely confront the persecution of Jesus, even to the point of death. In the Scriptures the word **"Life"** is often used to show a relationship that is right with God. It was Jesus who said, **"I have come that they may have *Life* and they may have it more abundantly."** Jesus provides us with what is required for our spiritual lives. He is the one who provides "living water." He is the bread of life. We know that our earthly lives will someday end, but, we have the amazing promise that comes only to those who come to God through Jesus. And this promise is what He offers, --- ***eternal life.***

James tells us that this crown of life is for all who love God. The question then is how do we demonstrate our love of God? The apostle John answers the question: **"For this is the love of God, "That we keep His commandments. To love one another, obeying Him always, and remaining faithful."** So as we endure the inevitable trials, the pain, the heartache and burdens, as long as we live we look forward to seeing Jesus, the author and finisher of our faith, and receive the **Crown of Life** that awaits us.

WHO SEES OUR WORTH

"Our hearts may condemn us." With those words, the Bible acknowledges that a times our heart may cause us to be overly critical of ourselves. Indeed, it may insist that we are unworthy of God's love and care. Yet, the Bible reassures us: **"God is greater than our hearts and knows all things." 1 John 3:19, 20.**

God knows us better than we know ourselves. He views us in a very different way, than the way we view ourselves. What then are we worth in the eyes of the one who really matters—Jehovah God?

The answer can be found in a touching illustration that Jesus used on two separate occasions. Jesus said that, "Two sparrows sell for a coin of small value." **Matthew 10:29, 31.** According to **Luke 12: 6, 7,** Jesus also said: *"Five sparrows sell for two coins of small value,"* yet not one of them goes forgotten before God. . *"Have no fear, you are worth more than many sparrows"* This simple but powerful illustration teaches us how God views each of His worshippers.

In Biblical time sparrows were among the cheapest of all birds used for food. Jesus observed poor women, perhaps even his own mother, in the marketplace buying these tiny birds to feed to their families. The birds were so inexpensive that for two coins, **one coin was worth less than five cents in modern value,** a buyer could purchase two sparrows. For two coins the buyer received not four but five sparrows at no additional cost.

Jesus explained that not a single sparrow goes forgotten before God, or falls the ground without the Father's knowledge. Matthew 10:29. The seemingly insignificant birds that were not too little for

Jehovah to create are not too little for Him to remember. In fact He values them for they are precious living things. And so it is with us.

In light of Jesus' words, we need not feel that we are too unworthy to be noticed and cared for by the God who is **"greater than our hearts."** Isn't it comforting to know that our Creator may see **in us** what we may not be able to see in ourselves? We need to know that we will not be remembered by our words, but by our kind deeds. Life is not measured by the number of breathes we take but by the moments that take our breath.

In the light of Jesus words, we need not feel that we are too unworthy to be noticed and cared for the God who is **"Greater than our hearts."** Isn't it comforting to know that our Creator may see in us what we may not be able to see in ourselves? We need to know that we won't be remembered by what we say as much as we will be remembered by our deeds. Life is not measured by the breaths we take but rather by the moments that take our breath.

WE CAN'T FOOL GOD

Praying is like breathing, it is easier to do than not do it. We pray for a variety of reasons. What sin did Jesus condemn more than any other sin? **Hypocrisy.** Especially the flagrant self-congratulatory kind that was practiced by the religious leaders of His day. Religious hypocrites are unspiritual shams. They are always looking to gain respect by playing the role of God-lovers by appearing to obey His law but they are often times unholy fakes who try to fool people, but they can't fool God. In Jesus time they were called Sadducees and Pharisees, members of the Sanhedrin. They wanted people to believe that they were very special religious leaders and acutely righteous. In a convocation address, Luther Smith, a professor at Emory University's School of Theology, warned against the danger of ""faking it"----pretending to be something we are not. He mentioned that he had seen a bumper sticker that read, **"Jesus is coming! Look Busy."** Although we may think that we are **looking busy** we cannot fool God about our faith, our character or our service. Like the Pharisees, whom Jesus denounced in Matthew 23: 13-15. He warned them, *"But woe be to you scribes and hypocrites, because you shut the Kingdom of heaven against men; for you neither enter yourselves, nor allow those who would enter to go in. Woe to you scribes for you traverse sea and land to make a single proselyte, and when he becomes a proselyte you make him twice as much a child of hell, as yourselves."* Matthew 23: 13-15. The word proselyte is a Greek word which means, *"Come Unto."* It's found only four times in the New

Testament. The term was used very loosely in the 1ˢᵗ Century by the Jews when referring to worshippers who had been converted.

We may appear to be sincerely religious but the Lord knows our feelings if they are merely a facade without saving trust and genuine devotion. Our intentions need to be true and righteous. Are we churchgoing hypocrites, depending on our won good works to gain entrance into heaven or do we trust God's grace by relying on Jesus Christ? **You can't fool God, It's not enough to look busy.** What can we do? Every Christian can maintain a prayer life. Why pray? What is the point of prayer when God knows the future and is already in control? Praying is like breathing, it is easier to do than not to do. We pray for a variety of reasons:

Praying is a form of serving God. Luke 2:36-38.
Praying is a form of obeying God.
Praying is a command given to us by God. Philippians 4:6-7
Prayer was taught to us by Jesus Christ and the early Church.

If Jesus thought it was worthwhile to pray, we should pray. If He needed to pray to remain in His Father's will how much more do we need to pray as Christians? Prayer works:

God intends prayer to be the means of obtaining His solutions.

Pray in preparation for major decisions it is essential. Luke 6:12-13

Pray to overcome demonic barriers works. Matthew 17:14-21

Pray to gather workers for the spiritual harvest it is important. Lk.10:2

Pray to overcome temptation it is positive. Matthew 26:41

We come to God with our specific requests, and we have God's promise that our prayers are not in vain, even if we do not receive specifically what we ask for. He promises that when we ask for things that are in accordance with His will, He will give us what we ask for. Sometimes He delays His answers according to His wisdom and for our benefit. In these situations we are to be diligent and persistent in prayer. Prayer should not be seen as our means of getting God to do our will on earth, but rather as a means of getting God's will done on earth. God's wisdom far exceeds our own.

Remember, **"You Can't Fool God. It is not enough to look busy."**

God sees our ways and knows our hearts,
From Him we cannot hide.
External righteousness can't save,
For He knows what's left inside.

ON WHOM DO WE RELY?

If you are looking for practical ways to live your life as a Christian then you should turn to the book of James, in the New Testament, because the author James, Jesus' disciple shows that it is possible to believe the right things yet live the wrong way.

No one knows for sure which James wrote this scripture. Most believe that it was James, Jesus' brother. It is a very short book, it contains only five chapters. James may have been the first New Testament book to be written, between 40 AD and 50 AD. The letter takes a no-nonsense approach to hypocrisy. James describes the evil of a tongue out of control, showing favoritism toward the rich and boosting about plans for tomorrow. It is a book that addresses a string of hard-hitting, specific, practical instructions to help us live an authentic Christian life.

Jesus said, *"Here on earth you will have many trials."* John 16:33. We solve one problem, and another comes along to take its place. They are not all big, but they're all necessary to our spiritual growth. How do we assess the strength of something? By testing it. The Bible says, *"Don't be shocked that you are going through testing, for the testing prepares you."* Some of our most life-enriching experiences come during our worst moments; when your heart is broken, when you feel abandoned, when it seems like you are out of options, when your pain levels go through the roof. You turn to God and that is when you learn to pray heartfelt, honest-to-God prayers. James says, *"Humble yourselves under God's mighty hand, that he may lift you up in due time. Cast all of your anxiety on him because he care for you."* James 5:6.

God could have kept Joseph out of prison, Daniel out of the lion's den, Jeremiah out of the slimy pit and Paul from being ship wrecked, but he didn't. As a result each of them was drawn closer to God and as a result impacted the world around them.

Our problems force us to look to God and depend on him instead of ourselves. And that is good! James encourages us to be patient. He illustrates his point by referring to the farmer who waits for the land to yield its valuable crop. He must patiently wait for the autumn and spring rains before harvest is completed.

As my children grew up I remember a time when I was forced to show patience and understanding with one of my boys. Shane was an independent, hard headed little five year old who believed he could always do it himself. If was tough to try to help him unless he thought he needed help. One day he was trying to put on his jacket. He yanked at the jacket attempting to fasten the zipper. He was frustrated by his inability, but refused any offers of help. I just left him alone to work out his problem.

Finally, Shane came to me and asked, "Hey Dad can you help me with this zipper?" As I knelt to zip my son's coat I realized how much like him that I am. I have resisted calling on God for help, childishly convinced that I could do it myself. How many times had God waited on me to cry "uncle" so that he could come and rescue me? How foolish to rely on my own strength and ingenuity when I have access to the vast storehouse of Go's wisdom and ability. On whom do we rely?

God, your ways are always superior to mine. I will henceforth call on you rather than wait until I have used up all my options.

A SMALL GESTURE MAY
MAKE A BLESSING

Many people pass through our lives but only **real friends** leave their imprints on our heart. Our scripture reading is found in Psalm 100: 5, as David sings about praising God. *"For the Lord is good; His steadfast love endures forever and He is faithful to all generations."* Psalm 100: 5

An act of goodness that you do today may come back to you, or someone you love, as a blessing when you least expect it. And so it is with Christians who reach out to help others. A small gesture, a thoughtful act, an unselfish expression, a friendly smile a compliment, or a pat on the back, all work miracles when righteously done. Let me share with you a story about a seemingly small gesture that certainly became a blessing.

One day a young boy named Howard, was going door to door selling home goods and cleaning supplies. He didn't have much money, his parents were poor. Howard was working to pay for his education. As he went along knocking on doors and talking with home owners, and selling his wares he became very hungry. He only had 10 cents in his pocket so he decided he should ask someone for some food.

The next house that he came to was a big beautiful Victorian house. It was well maintained, with many flowers and shrubs around a perfectly manicured lawn. Certainly someone with money must live there. He went up to the front door and rang the bell. An attractive young girl greeted him with a smile. He forgot about being hungry and asked the girl if he could have a drink of water.

The girl thought that Howard looked very hungry so she went to the kitchen and instead of water she returned with glass of milk. He drank it very slowly savoring every drop. When he had finished he ask, "How much do I owe you?" "You don't owe me anything." she replied, "My mother taught me never to accept anything for doing something kind for someone in need."

Howard grinned and said, "Then I thank you from the bottom of my heart." When Howard Kelly left the house he was refreshed. He had a renewed feeling of physical strength and he sensed a return of his faith in the Lord. He had been so busy working to earn money for school he had nearly abandoned his faith.

Years went by. The same young woman who gave Howard a glass of milk, fell gravely ill. Her personal physician was mystified. He called on his associates and it was decided that she should go to the big city where they knew there was a specialist who would be able to diagnose the rare disease and possibly help her.

Doctor Howard Kelly was called as a consultant. When he heard the name of the town in which the woman lived, a memory burned brightly in his eyes. He went directly to the woman's room. He recognized her and went back to his office determined to do the best he could to save her life. From that day on he paid special attention to the case, monitoring her progress every day. After a long battle, the woman recovered.

Dr. Kelly left instructions that the bill for this woman's care should be sent to him for his review. When he received it he looked it over, wrote something in the margin and put it in an envelope, sealed it and instructed the staff to leave it in the woman's room.

When the woman opened the envelope she found an invoice, in detail, and she shuttered thinking it would take her the rest of her life to pay it in full. As she scanned the bill something caught her attention. In the margin of the invoice she read these words, **"Paid-In-Full, with a glass of milk."** Signed, Howard Kelly MD.

Tears of joy filled her eyes and touched her heart. She prayed, *"Thank you Lord for your love which has crossed the heart and hands of man."*

If you receive a blessing pass it on. A blessing cannot be kept. If it stops with the recipient the blessing disappears. If we receive a blessing we need to keep it working. Be the source of a blessing to other people.

The hardest lesson in life is to know which bridges to cross and which to burn.

Do We Have Time for God

We all receive e-mails from time to time. Sometimes it seems as though we receive more than we need or want. Have you gone to your "in box" and found a number of messages that you feel were too much trouble to answer? Your reaction was probably one of, "I don't have time for this." Or perhaps you simply deleted every one you saw and felt that it was an imposition of someone you probably don't even know and who was inappropriate for having bothered you with all of that non-sense.

Then, I suggest that this might be the kind of thinking that has caused a lot of problems in our world today. We want to be selective when responding and we want to be able to do it at our convenience, so it doesn't put us to any extra effort.

Too often we do this with our relationship with God. We try to keep God in our Church on Sunday morning, during worship hour, and in Sunday school... or even Sunday evening, but we hit the delete key during the rest of the week. We like to have God around during sickness, when we are in the hospital or the nursing home or if we are bereaved. We certainly want to have Him present at our weddings and our funerals.

But too often we don't have enough time, or room for Him during our work or play time. May God forgive me for ever thinking that there is a time or a place where His is not welcome or isn't first **in my life.**

We should always have time to remember all that He has done for us. If you are ashamed to admit this, then you need to know what Jesus said, *"If you are ashamed of me, I will be ashamed of you before my father."*

Promise not to be ashamed. Tell others that you know God through His son Jesus Christ. Tell God that you love Him and that you know Him through Jesus. He is the source of our existence and the promise of ever-lasting life. God keeps us functioning each and every day. Without him we would be nothing. *"With Christ he strengthens me." Phil 4:13. NIV*

Not long ago I received a letter from an old friend. Jim was reminiscing about the wonderful times we had at the summer Boy Scout Camp that we worked at as counselors while we were going to school. His letter was long and detailed. He named person after person and recalled many events that I had long forgotten. It brought back a flood of memories. He mentioned nearly thirty of our co-workers and said something positive about each one.

It caused me to ponder the impact of my words. I asked myself, "Does what I say about someone bring encouragement and affirmation?" Am I usually talking about what's wrong or what is right? Am I primarily positive or negative?

Proverbs 10:11 describes the mouth of the righteous as a well of life. It calls the tongue of the righteous, choice silver. The lips of the righteous feed many. The two things that are constants are: (a) the person who is righteous----right with God deep inside, and, (b) words that nourish and refresh others.

Jesus, our Savior, spoke life-giving words. We can encourage and lift the spirits of others today by what we say to them and what we say about them.

Gracious Spirit, dwell with me:
I would always gracious be;
For righteous words that help and heal
Then Thy life in mine reveals.

A well-chosen word can speak volumes.

"Let your light so shine before others that they may see your good works and glorify God in heaven." Matthew 5:16

Are You Being Tempted

No matter how spiritual you become, or how spiritually mature you might think you are, you never outgrow temptation. When you meet one temptation head on, and overcome it, you will often find another one hits you from behind. It seems like the more you resist temptation the more difficult it becomes.

Temptation is a part of life. No one is immune to temptation---at any age. For temptation is present whenever there is a choice to be made, not only between good or evil, but also between a higher or lower case of **good**. For some, it may be a temptation for sensual gratification; for others a temptation to misuse their gifts, to seek personal success at the cost of general welfare. Or to seek a worthy aim by unworthy means, and to lower their ideals and standards in order to win favor with their companions or associates.

Even the closer you get to God the more Satan tries to tempt you. Paul explains it this way:

The sinful nature wants to do evil . . . which is just the opposite of what the Father, Son and the Holy Spirit want you to do. These two forces are constantly fighting each other. In Galatians 5: 17 Paul explains it this way: "*...let no one cause me trouble, for I bear on my body the marks of Jesus.*" Paul had often been beaten for the sake of Jesus. Even those living in Galatia could recall how Paul had nearly died in order to get the message of the gospel to them.

Jesus Christ was tempted. In the Gospel of Mark the scripture records Jesus' temptations Mk. 1: 12-13. Luke gives a detailed account of Jesus' temptations in Luke 4: 1-13. Matthew provides another account of temptations in Mt. 4:1-10.

The scriptures tell of how the Holy Spirit lead Jesus into the wilderness and Jesus fasted for 40 days and 40 nights. Satan came to Jesus and began to tempt him. In Jesus' hungered condition the devil asked him to turn two stones to bread. Jesus replied, "Man does not live by bread alone." Then the devil took Jesus to the

Holy city and stood at the highest point. He asked Jesus to cast himself down and suggested that the angels would save him before he reached the ground. Jesus' answer was, "Do not put the Lord your God to the test." Then the devil took Jesus to the highest mountain where he could see all of the Kingdoms of the world. The devil again tempted Jesus by saying, "If you worship me I will give all that you see to you." Jesus answered, "Worship the Lord your God and serve him only."

Why would the Holy Spirit lead Jesus into the wilderness to be tempted by Satan? In order for Christ to accomplish God's will, he had to face the devil, be tempted by him and finally prevail. Jesus had to win out, be successful, and when tempted by Satan, win. Matthew presents Jesus as the one who served faithfully despite enormous opposition. Jesus' confrontation with Satan shows that temptation doesn't need to end in failure. Similarly, God may allow our faith to be tested on the path to spiritual success. As we rely on God's help to win battles over temptation, we become more and more prepared to fulfill the purpose God has given us.

So what is the answer? Here are **two ways** that you can overcome temptation: **(1)** be honest about it. Ask yourself this question: "**When am I tempted most?**" Usually we are most vulnerable when we are under stress, or when we are hurt, or angry; when we are worried, alone, bored or tired. Perhaps even when we have had a big success or a spiritual high, and we are just getting over it. Learn to recognize your patterns. God's people protect themselves by watching were they go and what they do. ***"When a man's ways are pleasing to the***

*Lord, he makes even his enemies live at peace with him." Prov.
16: 7.*

(2) **Reach** out for help. Call on the Lord for his help. **Psalm 50:
15** says, *"....call upon me in the day of trouble, I will deliver you
and you will honor me."* So why don't we call on God more often?
Maybe we are embarrassed because we just want to do what we want
to do. Perhaps it is because we keep giving in to the same temptations
and just can't resist any longer. Don't be discouraged, God won't
Give up on you. His word says, *"Approach the throne of grace with
confidence So that you may receive mercy and find grace to help
in your time of need."* **Heb. 4: 16.** If you have to cry out for God's
help every hour of the day or night, He will be there for you just as
the roots of a tree deepen when the storms come, each time you stand
up to temptation you become stronger.

Once there was a wise old Indian Chief who had a young son who
was growing up and seeking answers to many of life's problems. The
old Chieftain invited his son to join him in his tepee. They sat quietly
near the fire watching the burning embers slowly fade. Finally, the
old Chief began to tell his son this story:

"In each of us live two wolves. Both wolves are very strong and
fierce. However, the first wolf is a **bad wolf**. He cannot be trusted.
He steals from his brother. He is very impatient and unkind. He is
disrespectful. Easily tempted and very selfish.

The second wolf is a **good wolf.** He is trustworthy, and helpful.
He is courteous and kind. He is obedient and a very happy wolf. The
problem is the two wolves are constantly competing and fighting with
one another to take over your person.

The old Chief paused and didn't say another word. No one spoke
until finally the young brave asked: **"Which wolf wins?"** The Chief
answered: **"The one you feed."**

MAKING A CHANGE

Taking Chances. We all take chances. Sometimes taking a chance is a voluntary action. We have a choice. By doing a certain thing we believe that we will gain by taking a chance. Flip a coin. Heads or tails? The odds are fifty-fifty either way. However, making a bet, or a wager, or taking a chance may be another matter and it may be difficult to determine the odds. . We may even consider it a gamble and all gambles have risk. Someone wins but often times they lose. It is usually wise to know what the risks are before we chose to gamble.

When it comes to our life style or well-being we normally don't like to take a risk. Often we are faced with situations that we cannot avoid. For situations that are avoidable we often do not like to make a change, so it becomes status-quo.

We have all heard the term, **"March Madness."** The first thing that comes to mind is the craziness that goes on at the end of the basketball season. It starts with the end of the normal competitive season, about March 1st, and we are thrust into the games and tournaments that determine the champions of the various leagues and divisions, from the grammar school level to the University teams. They all compete for their respective trophies and national recognition.

There is another kind of **"March Madness,** one that we all experience. If you feel like you have had enough of winter and gray days, ice and snow, and are feeling a little low or depressed you are part of the majority. Most of us tend to eat and sleep a little more in the winter and we experience more ups and downs during the shorter days. Winter may bring about some weight gain and lack of energy for people in general. For some, the dark days and cold temperatures result in a type of clinical depression known as **Seasonal Affective Disorder. (SAD).** For this we would definitely like to make a change.

SAD is usually experienced from October through March and is thought to be directly related to body temperature and the eye's exposure to light. Some symptoms in addition to those mentioned may include:

> Lack of energy and loss of interest in work or activities.
> Slow, sluggish, lethargic movement.
> Social withdrawal.
> Unhappiness and irritability.

While symptoms usually disappear with the coming of spring and summer there are some ways to minimize their affects: Exercise regularly, eat healthy foods, get exposed to sunlight and keep your mind occupied by reading good books, listening to music, even reading the Bible. Scripture tell us: *"...stand firm. Let nothing move you. Give yourselves fully to the work so the Lord, because you know that your labor in the Lord is not in vain".* 1 Cor. 15:58 NIV

Don't get caught up in **March Madness,** spring is just around the corner.

DID JESUS EVER LAUGH

There has long been a notion that Jesus never laughed. We look at pictures and painting of Jesus and traditionally we see a somber, glum, melancholy portrayal of a man who seems to be depressed and downhearted. It is true that Jesus became our **Sin-bearer.** But, He was rejected and despised by mankind. He was a man of suffering and was familiar with pain. Jesus was rejected in His hometown, He wept twice, once at the graveside of Lazarus. He did not weep over the death itself because He knew that Lazarus would be raised and would spend eternity with Him in heaven. But, Jesus could not help but weep when confronted by Lazarus's Sisters Mary and Martha who were wailing and sobbing along with the other mourners. Jesus wept again when He entered Jerusalem on Palm Sunday. He said, *"O Jerusalem, Jerusalem, the city that kills the prophets and stones those sent to her! How often I wanted to gather your children together, just as a hen gathers her brood under her wings, and you would not have it." Luke 13:34.* Jesus cried aloud in anguish over the future of the city. Jesus knew that in 40 years more than a million residents of Jerusalem would die in one of the most gruesome sieges in recorded history.

The picture of Jesus we find in the Gospels; Matthew, Mark, Luke and John, is one of a well-rounded, magnetic personality. He was accused of being too joyful on occasion. *"The Son of Man came eating and drinking, and you say, 'Here is a glutton and a drunkard, a friend of tax collectors and sinners.' Luke 7: 34.* Jesus carried children around in His arms---What child wants to be close to a person who is an old grump and never smiles?

As the Son of Man, Jesus shared the full human experience. We cannot imagine life without laughter; even when we are in dire circumstances we have seasons of joy. Everyone laughs and appreciates good humor. An old clique says, **"Laughter is our best medicine."** To say that Jesus never expressed joy through laughter is akin to denying His full humanity.

Jesus encouraged joyful laughter, most famously in the **Beatitudes,** recorded in Matthew 5 and Luke 6. Jesus said, ***"Blessed are you who weep now, for you shall laugh."*** Jesus spoke of rejoicing in His parables in Luke 15; the lost coin, the lost son, were all found. The result in each case was great rejoicing. Even more telling is that Jesus told these stories as illustrations of ***"joy before the angels of God over one who repents."*** Luke 15:10.

Jesus evinced a sense of humor in His teaching when He spoke of the ***"log in one's eye."*** *a purposeful exaggeration, and* the one of *"the camel going through the eye of a needle."*

Jesus had a serious mission to accomplish in this world. But, He was not somber all of the time. There is no verse in the Bible that says Jesus laughed, but we do know that He emphasized with us completely and felt all of our emotions. Laughter is a part of life and Jesus truly lived.

There is a time to laugh and a time to weep. We do not crack jokes in the presence of those who have just lost a close friend, a relative or a loved one. Silly jokes are out of place on such occasions. In the same way Jesus is focused on the lost and is looking for those who will care for their souls as He does. That is why our lives (while having times of refreshing humor) are to be characterized by soberness. God bless us in our witness.

MANY FACES OF HAPPINESS

I've been feeling a little grumpy lately. Maybe it is due to the weather. The ice and snow and associated gray days with a power outage thrown in for good measure. It has made New England a difficult place to live this winter. Included in the list are a few more pressures that we have had, like; Heating the house and paying for the heating oil, maintaining the vehicles in the extreme cold temperatures; Keeping the walkways and driveways clear of ice and snow; just getting out to do the grocery shopping turns into a major production. And I am certain that we all could add many more discomforts to the list, if we tried. So, the question is: "What can we do about it?" My friend suggested, "Take it or leave it." We could go to Florida or Arizona, or another warm weather location, and leave winter behind. That may or may not be practical. Or, we may have to do like other New Englanders have done for centuries, endure it.

The scripture has a suggestion: *"A happy heart makes the face cheerful." Proverbs 15:13.* If we can find a person with a happy face and talk with them we may discover their secret for a happy heart. Find out what makes them so content. How can they be leading a charmed life while others seem to be struggling? You may find out one reason is their relationship with their family. Their family loves them. They are comfortable at home even when the winter squalls occur.

Perhaps it is their Church, which combined with faith, gives them an abiding feeling of optimism that whatever may happen they have a strong spiritual life and they know that God loves them. Having a sense of purpose makes for a **happy heart**. Helping others to know the Lord is rewarding and gratifying. And, oh yes, a **sense of humor.** Humor has been defined as, ***"The sunshine of the mind and the harmony of the heart."*** If you can't laugh about the journey you won't be able to endure the ups and downs.

Happiness is the result of being **too busy** to be miserable. Try to stay active. Stay involved as long as you can. If you enjoy reading, that activity has wonderful rewards. Obviously, physical exercise is beneficial. Keep your mind and body busy and be happy.

Visit with your friends and peers. Ask them what it is that makes them happy and if you are challenged by their answers, try them.

Several years ago I was based at NAS Saufley Field, Pensacola, Florida. I was a Naval Aviation Cadet working on earning my Navy Wings of Gold. I was in the formation flying phase, close to completing it and looking forward to Gunnery School and then carrier qualifications. Before we finished at Saufley we had to make a formation, cross-country flight. Four cadets and their instructor had to fly a four legged course, with each cadet leading a leg. If we passed the check ride we would move on to Barren Field, gunnery and CQ. (Carrier Qualification)

The day came and we met at the hanger with our instructor. The instructor's name was Cook Cleland. I didn't realize it immediately but as I tried to recall the name I remembered who Cook Cleland was. He was a Navy pilot who during the early part of WWII became a hero by sinking a Japanese aircraft carrier in the Pacific with his SBD Dauntless dive bomber. He was awarded the Navy Cross, Air Medal with three Gold Stars, the Purple Heart, a Navy Commendation and a Presidential Citation. I was overwhelmed! LCDR Cleland was as nice a man as you would ever meet. He was happy, and his face showed it. I wanted to ask him a 'hundred questions but the other pilots were anxious to get on with the flight so we finished the briefing and launched.

The flight was a text book flight. The only flaw was as the second pilot led the formation northward into Alabama he suddenly realized he didn't know where he was. He was lost. He was afraid he was going to overshoot the turn point and fail the check-ride.. When LCDR Cleland asked the leader his position the cadet fearfully admitted he was confused, so Cleland instructed the formation to maintain their altitude and heading and he would be right back. I watched as he peeled off and dove down toward a little town below. It wasn't long before he was back in formation and when we asked what he had done, he said, "I just buzzed that little town and got the name off the water tower. It is Mt. Vernon, Alabama. Each cadet looked at his chart and we all knew exactly where we were. The flight continued and we completed the final check ride with a passing score. When we got back to Flight Operations, LCDR Cleland bought us each a cold drink and we had a great de-briefing.

I have often wondered what might have happened if we hadn't had a happy instructor like LCDR Cleland. A man who became a legend in the world of aviation. Many a pilot remembers him as an industry leader and a happy man. I never learned his church affiliation or much more about him but I do know of his deep respect and his love of Naval Aviation.

James 5: 13 says: *"Is any one of you in trouble? He should pray. Is anyone happy! Let him sing songs of praise."*

THE GOOD SAMARITAN

Luke 10: 25-37 NIV

Jesus used many ways to teach and to explain to the people the righteous way of life. One method Jesus used was to make an example using a parable to convey the message. A parable is an earthly story with a heavenly meaning.

Jesus was meeting with a group of people, one of which was an expert in the Law. The man stood up and said, *"Teacher, what must I do to inherit eternal life?"* Jesus in his special way answered the question with a question. He said, "What is written in the Law? How do you read it?"

The man answered: *"Love the Lord your God with all of your heart and with all of your soul and with all your strength and with all of your mind; and Love your neighbor as yourself."* Jesus confirmed, "Do this and you will live."

But the man was not satisfied and wanted to justify himself. So he asked Jesus, *"And who is my neighbor?"* Jesus began the parable:

"A man was going down from Jerusalem to Jericho when he fell into the Hands of robbers. They stripped him of his clothes, beat him and went away leaving him for dead. A priest happen to be going down the same road and when he saw the man, he passed him by on the other side. So too, a Levite when he came to the place and saw him and passed by on the other side. But a Samaritan, as he traveled, came where the man was and when he saw him he took pity on him. He went to him and bandaged his wounds, pouring oil and wine on him. He put the man on his donkey and took him to an Inn to care for him. The next day he took out two silver coins and gave them to the Innkeeper with instructions to look after the man and said that when he returned he would reimburse him for any extra expense

Jesus then asked the expert in Law, "Which of these three men do think was a neighbor to the man who fell into the hands of the robbers?" The man replied. *"The one who had mercy on him,"* Jesus told him, "Go and do likewise."

Can you see yourself in this parable? How would you have reacted? Would you have done what the priest and the Levite did, cross over to the other side of the road and not get involved?

Reflecting on the parable we need to understand that people in those days did not wish to get involved with a Samaritan. Samaritans were not well liked. They were to be avoided by all means. What would be our reaction today if we were faced with having to make a decision based on race, color or creed or ethnic back ground?

The Good Samaritan had to reach out to help the man in distress. He had to trust the innkeeper enough to leave the injured victim in his care. The innkeeper had to believe that the Samaritan would return and pay him for any extra expenses he incurred, as promised.

We often go through life looking for ways to follow Jesus, but I wonder if we are willing to extend our selves in the way that the Good Samaritan did in this story. Jesus wants us to be like the Good Samaritan. In other words, like Jesus. Which means acting without thought of reward, but being motivated by pure love and not counting the cost.

What we must do is to embrace our Savior and ask the Holy Spirit to enable us to venture forth beyond our comfort zone and enter the realm of joyful service.

**"Jesus said to the man who wanted to be justified,
'Go and do likewise.' Luke 10: 37 NIV**

NO ORDINARY DAY

When my children were young and were still at home, we lived in a house located in Bloomfield, Connecticut. We had about three acres of land and a small brook meandered through the back section. It wasn't deep enough to swim in and there weren't any fish to catch but the brook was home to hundreds of tadpoles who by the 4th of July each year were considered fair game for our annual 4th of July Family Picnic and Frog Jumping Contest.

It was a tradition for the boys, and their father, to go out in the morning of the 4th, before the guests arrived, and with a couple of nets we would catch twenty or thirty frogs and put them in several large plastic buckets. We were careful not to harm the frogs. There is nothing more frustrating than to get a handicapped frog for the big frog jumping contest.

About noon time the guests would start to arrive, the picnic began with all of the food and embellishments, and we enjoyed all. A Red, White and Blue celebration including cherry pie, blue berry pie and vanilla ice-cream.

Then it came time for the big event. No fireworks, sparklers or fire crackers. It was time for the Frog Jumping Contest. All of the children would line up on a line, parallel to the brook, at a distance of about forty feet, and wait to get their frog. Each person had a large paper cup and the officials would carry the bucket of frogs down the line and put a frog under each cup. With a Ready, Set, Go, the contest began. At the command Go, the paper cup was lifted and the race was on.

The rules were simple: No one could touch the frog, kick it, or pick it up and throw it. You could get down on your knees and yell at the frog. You could slap the ground behind it to make it jump towards the brook. You might even try blowing on its rump. Anything to make it move. The object was to have your frog get back into the water first. One year we had enough kids that we ran several heats, with the final winners receiving a first, second and third prize.

But, you can't imagine the things that happened. One little girl lifted her cup, released the frog and the critter jumped right back into her lap. You can imagine the reaction and horror that resulted. One of the kids had a frog who wouldn't move.

It must have been traumatized by all of the confusion. One of the boys was trying to get his frog to jump by pounding on the ground behind it. It wouldn't go quickly enough so the boy began to stomp on the ground behind it. Oops, a misjudged stomp smashed the frog into the turf. That required a replacement frog.

One year we had an exceptionally dry spring. The brook was almost dry. No frogs in sight. What could we do? Not far from the house was a small pond so we went to the pond to catch frogs. Armed with nets and buckets we expected to catch at least a few little critters. We were successful, we got a dozen or so. Some were even larger and more active than the ones we had in our brook. That was a fun day because we had to run several heats, catching the frogs that made it to the brook and running them again in the next race, three or four times. By the end of the day we had some pretty worn out frogs. It was no ordinary day for the frogs, and certainly no ordinary day for the kids, and the adults as well. And so it was.

"How great is the love the Father has lavished on us, that we should be called children of God! And that is what we are." 1 John 3:1a (NIV)

There are no **Ordinary Days** for a child of God. We are daily lavished with God's extraordinary love and grace. Trusting, childlike eyes see wonders showered on us even in the most unexpected places.

The Apostle Paul wrote a letter to the Church at Corinth. A new church that he had started some two to three years prior. He was concerned for them because he heard reports of strife and division threatening the young church. Some had become spirituality arrogant leading to misconduct against other believers. Paul wrote seeking to restore balance to the church.

In chapter 13: 4-7, Paul reminds us of our relationship with God and explains the love we have and how it works.

Love

> *"Love is patient, love is kind. It does*
> *not envy, it does not boast.*
> *It is not proud. It is not rude. It is not self-*
> *seeking. It is not easily angered.*
> *It keeps no record of wrongs. Love does not delight in evil*
> *But rejoices with the truth. It always protects, always trusts.*
> *Always hopes, and always perseveres."*
> *1 Corinthians 13: 4-7*

THE VIRGIN BIRTH

Heaven announced the birth of Jesus in these words: "The virgin will give birth to a son, and call him Immanuel, which means **God is with us.**" Isn't it ironic even with all of the prophesying and the scriptures contained in the Old Testament and by the word that Isaiah proclaimed there was still doubt? Isaiah said, "For to us a child is born, for to us a son is given, and the government will be on his shoulders. And he will be called wonderful counselor, Mighty God, Everlasting Father, Prince of Peace. Of the increase of his government and peace there will be no end. He will reign on David's throne and over his kingdom, establishing it and upholding it with justice and righteousness from that time on and forever." Isaiah 9: 6-7. Isaiah wrote these words about 970 BC years before Christ was born.

The leaders of Israel, the religious right, the Pharisees, the educated, the establishment, said to Jesus: "We were not born of fornication." (James 8: 41) Their insinuation was clear and very Cruel. After all, Jesus could not point to Joseph and say "He is my father." Understand this, Jesus had to be **man** in order to die, and he had to be **God** in order to save. If you were a child of an earthly father you were born in sin. But Jesus was born of a heavenly Father so he broke the genetic cycle of sin even before he was born.

In the Old Testament a sacrificial lamb had to be without blemish (birth defect) or spot something picked up along the way. Since Jesus had neither inherited sin, nor practiced sin He qualifies as "**The Lamb of God**" and was able to take away the sins of the world." (John 1: 29)

87

The virgin birth is true because (a) the angel of the Lord announced it. Matthew 1: 20 (b) Mary's revelation and (c) Mary's espoused husband Joseph, accepted it. (Matthew 1: 24). (c) Mary's cousin, Elizabeth received the word by divine revelation, (Luke 1: 41-42). Thus as we read the scriptures written by Luke, the physician, we know the certainty of the things that we have been taught.

Luke 2: 4-20 tells the story of the virgin birth. "So Joseph also went up from the town of Nazareth in Galilee to Judea, to Bethlehem the town of David, because he belonged to the house and the line of David. He went there to register with Mary, who was pledged to be his wife and was expecting a child. While they were there the time came for the baby to be born, and she gave birth to her firstborn, a son. She wrapped him in cloths and placed him a manger, because there was no room for them in the inn.

And there were shepherds living out in the fields nearby, keeping watch over their flocks at night. An angel of the Lord appeared to them, and the glory of the Lord shone around them, and they were terrified. But the angel said to them, "Do not be afraid. I bring you good news of great joy that will be for all of the people. Today in the town of David a Savior has been born to you; he is Christ the Lord. This will be a sign to you; you will find a baby wrapped in cloths and lying in a manger."

Suddenly a great company of heavenly host appeared with the angel praising God and saying, **"Glory to God in the highest and on earth peace to men on whom his favor rests."**

When the angels had left them and gone into heaven, the shepherds said to one another, "Let's go to Bethlehem and see this thing that has happened, which the Lord has told us about."

So they hurried off and found Mary and Joseph and the baby, who was lying in the manger. When they had seen him, they spread the word concerning what had been told them about this child, and all who heard it were amazed at what the shepherds said to them. But Mary treasured up all these things and pondered them in her heart. The shepherds returned, glorifying and praising God for all the things they had heard and seen, which were just as they had been told.

Christmas is the accommodation and the blessing of God to the world. Jesus came not to condemn or destroy the world but rather to provide a way to save us from our sins and have everlasting life.

WAYS TO UNLOCK THE BEST OF YOUR LIFE

George Burns, the renowned comedian, story teller and movie celebrity offered some good suggestions on ways to get the best out of life. He also has recommended some advice to speakers, lectures and preachers on how to improve their oratory. He suggests that speeches or sermons being delivered should start with a much focused anecdote that relates to the subject and end with a dramatic lesson that the recipients can understand and apply to their lives. Furthermore, the end of the message should be as close to the beginning as possible.

Using George Burns' advice I would like to share with you, **"How to Spread Happiness."** A key to getting the best out of your life is to **SMILE.** "The simplest and most reliable way to make someone smile is to smile at them," says Professor Marianne LaFrance, a teacher, author and professor of psychology at Yale University.

"Smiles are the most contagious kind of facial expression, even among people who don't know each other," LaFrance says. "That is because seeing a smile and showing a smile originates from the same area of the brain."

So you are skeptical . . . can you change the world by just smiling more often? LaFrance suggests that we try this experiment. For one day, vow Not to smile at anyone. The next day smile at every one you meet. The compare the two days. Chances are the second day will be one of the better days that you have had in a long time. Good luck with your experiment.

There are many who believe that Christianity must be very sober, without much fun, not many smiles and very little laughter. This certainly is not the case. God has made each of us with our many emotions so that we may experience and truly appreciate the entirely of His creation. He encourages us not only to find joy in the things He has given us but to find joy and laughter in His very presence. Psalm 16: 11 says, *"You have made known to me the path of life, you fill me with your joy in your presence, with eternal pleasures at our right hand."*

There has been a notion that Jesus never laughed. Traditionally, paintings of Jesus have tended toward the melancholy portrayal of a somber, glum, Savior. It is true that Jesus became our **Sin-bearer; that** he was despised and rejected by mankind, was a man of suffering, and familiar with pain. Jesus was rejected in his hometown of Nazareth, where he spent his boyhood. He wept at his friend Lazarus' gravesite in Bethany. He was saddened to see the condition of Jerusalem upon his entry into the city. He suffered and died on the cross at Cavalry.

However, this does not mean Jesus never had a lighthearted moment. The pictures of Jesus that we find in the Gospels is one of a well-rounded, magnetic personality who loved the people he met. He carried little children in His arms, and embraced his associates. What person wants to be around an old grump who never laughs or smiles? Luke accused Him of being too joyful on occasion. **". . . Behold a glutton and a drunkard, a friend of tax collectors and sinners! Yet wisdom is justified by all her children."** *Luke 7: 34-35.*

The fact that we have a sense of humor is understandable since we have been created in God's image. The existence of a litter of puppies, a pod of dolphins, a rookery of penguins, or a family of otters who like to enjoy life to the fullest by displaying their joy by being together and sharing each other's company.

As the Son of Man Jesus shares the full human experience, we cannot imagine life without laughter, even those who are in dire circumstances. We all know seasons of joy, everyone laughs and appreciates good humor, which often starts with a smile.

Jesus encourage joyful laughter, which is illustrated in the Beatitudes, recorded in Matthew 5 and Luke 6. Jesus said, *"Blessed are you who weep now, for you shall laugh."* Jesus spoke of rejoicing in His parables in Luke 15 . . . The lost sheep, the lost coin, and the lost son, all who were found, causing great rejoicing.

Jesus had a serious mission to accomplish in this world, but He was not one to be somber all of the time. There is no verse in the Bible that says that Jesus laughed, but we know that he empathized with us completely and felt all of our emotions. Laughter is part of life, and Jesus truly lived a righteous life.

> *"He that cometh from above all; He that is of the earth and speaketh of the earth; He that cometh from heaven is above all."* **John 3: 31.**

PRAISE THE LORD

The thought for the day is, *"Let the name of the Lord be praised both now and forever more."*

When I was growing up my mother would always say, **"Praise the Lord."** Even when we were waiting for the bus and the rain clouds were threatening, just as the bus came around the corner the first couple of rain drops began to fall, she would say, "Praise the Lord." As we finished up the dinner dishes, all washed and dried and put away she would say, "Praise the Lord." We always had a jig saw puzzle on the table at Christmas time and as the last piece of the puzzle was put in place, mom would say, **"Praise the Lord."**

As a teenager, it was driving me crazy. I promised myself that I would not be like that. It wasn't that I didn't want to give thanks to the Lord, but for every little thing, even things that I didn't feel I needed to be thankful for, mom would say. **"Praise the Lord."** Her saying it over and over again was annoying.

I didn't want to be a complainer, but the Lord knew that I needed to change. I needed to grow spiritually. Romans 5: 3-4, Paul taught that life's predicaments can produce godly character in us. But, our complaining hinders God's work. Then, I learned some interesting things:

> (1) My troubles and frustrations did not take
>   God by surprise. He is still in control.
> (2) God has a solution, a provision, or a gift
>   of wisdom to match my difficulty.

(3) I needed to pray affirming my faith in Him
and believing His loving purpose for me.
(4) I needed to have patience trusting God
to work His perfect will, and
(5) Praise Him---even before He acts.

I was just a teenager, but when I read the answers to solving my dilemma, I began to apply them, and things began to change. I always give thanks to the Lord for that which I receive from Him. I don't always give my thanks out loud, like Mom did, but the words are there constantly in my head. "Praise the Lord." My mother taught me by example to praise God in all things, just as the scriptures tell us to do.

As we now approach that time of year when our attention is focused on the events leading to Easter, we need to remember a basic truth and practice it. That is, **"Praise the Lord."**

Many Christians are very cognizant of the traditions and events leading up to **Easter** and are very compliant in observing them. Others have less interest and Easter is always on a Sunday that falls between March 22nd and April 25. This would rather spend their energies on getting a new Easter bonnet, a new dress, or clothes, and making certain that they have eggs to dye and chocolate Easter Bunnies for everyone in the family. Easter is April 20th. Originally, the festival was known as *Eostre* which was the name of an Anglo-Saxon goddess. In 325 AD the church ruled that Easter should be celebrated on the first Sunday after the full moon following the Vernal Equinox and it would become a time when all would commemorate the death, burial and resurrection of God's son Jesus. It is at this time we can rightly say, **"Praise the Lord."**

The early church started the custom of preparing the believers for that the special day of Easter. They taught that for 40 days before Easter there is time that Christians should prepare themselves by performing acts of penance, observing periods of fasting, avoiding festivities, and remembering that Jesus has absolved of our sins by being crucified, dying, being buried and on the third day rising from the grave. We call the period Lent. It is Easter that we celebrate the resurrection, the remission of sin and the promise of everlasting life.

Lord, we praise you today because you are the Lord of all. All things come to us from you. We thank for the promise of life eternal through your son Jesus Christ.

SPIRITUAL HOUSECLEANING

**"The Lord has rewarded me according
to my righteousness, according
To the cleanness of my hands in His sight." Ps. 18:24**

Who likes to clean house? About as many people who like liver and onions. House cleaning is a lot of work. As people reach the golden years they go through the procedure of down-sizing their living quarters, changing the way they live and reducing the amount of work and expense necessary to maintain their existing life style. The kids have all grown up, the need for five bedrooms has been reduced to one or two, and the cost of heating oil and electricity have increased the per capita cost to the point that folks feel they need to make a change.

Housecleaning is a job that is so disliked that even working men and women often rationalize to the point that they would rather pay someone else to do it rather than do it themselves. There are several types of housecleaning, however, there are some that have to be done by you personally.

It is absolutely amazing how much junk can be collected in our homes in a very short time. In just a few months' time we can collect enough to fill up the bureau chest in the bedroom and stuff the closet with articles of clothing that will only be worn once or twice. Some people develop a fetish for hats, or shoes, purses and Accessories. Junk is piled behind the door, or shoved under the bed out of sight. When the junk begins to interfere with normal activities like walking across the room, getting clean socks out of a drawer, or getting your coat out of the closet, even reaching the lawnmower in the garage, it's time to start discarding the unnecessary stuff that is in the way

This may have been the exordium of the church rummage sale. Each year in the spring, charities throughout the land sponsor rummage sales. One to three days of truculent effort is converted into making "One person's trash another person's treasure," which is gleefully hauled home to be stored in the attic. A rummage sale accomplishes two important objectives: (1) It cleans out the closets and empties, the bureau drawers, and (2) it allows the charities to raise money for special projects.

The same thing happens spiritually. We get so busy with life that we allow stress, doubt, fear and complacency to fill our lives, to accumulate and block out the communications that we have with the Lord. We try to rationalize by blaming others for it happening, but we need to take a look at having a spiritual rummage sale of our own.

Even in pre-exilic time God made a covenant with the Israelites in establishing the Day of Atonement. **Yom Hakkipurim** was the annual Day of Atonement when the high priest offered sacrifices for the sins of the nation. Lev. 23; 27; 25:9 describes it in great detail. It was the only fasting period required by Mosaic Law. It came in August, the tenth day of Tishri and was preceded by special Sabbaths. God initiated the Day of Atonement because of man's inability to receive full atonement for his sins. It was a day of great solemnity requiring the strictest conformity to the law.

The high priest sanctified himself by a ceremonial bath and the donning of white garments. He made atonement for himself and the other priests by sacrificing a bullock. A goat was chosen, by lot, for a sin offering for the people and was sacrificed before the congregation. Blood from the bullock and the goat was sprinkled on and around the mercy seat of the Holy of Holies after it had been sanctified by incense. A third goat, known as a scapegoat, was released into the wilderness as a "sin bearer to carry the sins of the people away.

After the second ceremony the high priest was required to change his garments again after a second ceremonial bath.

God wanted to simplify the act of atonement so he sent his only begotten son, Jesus, to be our scapegoat, if we choose. Jesus wants to take away all of the unnecessary stuff that we carry so that that we can be totally receptive to him. Let us be spiritually clean. We need to begin the task of spiritual housecleaning today.

GOD KNOWS OUR
WANTS AND NEEDS

Isaiah 65: 24 says, *"Before they call I will answer, while they are yet speaking I will hear."*

This story is one that actually happened to a missionary doctor working at a clinic in an orphanage in Kenya, Africa. The Doctor was working in the hospital unit helping a mother who was in labor. In spite of all that the hospital team could do, the mother died, leaving a premature newborn baby and a two year old frightened daughter. The doctor realized that they would have trouble keeping the baby alive because they had no incubator or electrical power to run one. They also had no special feeding facilities.

Although they lived near the equator the nights were often chilly with lots of drafts. One of the student midwifes went for a box they often used for such babies and cotton wool that the baby could be wrapped. Another midwife went to stoke up the fire and to fill a hot water bottle. She came back shortly in distress to say that in filling the bottle it had burst. (Rubber perishes easily in tropical climates). "It's our last hot water bottle!" she exclaimed, "We don't have another." "All right," said the doctor, "Put the baby as near the fire as you safely can and sleep between the baby and the door to keep it free from drafts. It is your job to keep the baby warm."

The following noon the doctor went to have prayers with the children in the orphanage. As usual, he suggested different things that they could pray about one was for the tiny baby. He explained that the problem was the need to have the baby warm and out of all drafts. The baby could easily die if it got the chills. He told them about the damaged hot water bottle and also about the two-year old sister, crying because her mother had died.

During the prayer time one ten-year old girl, Ruth, prayed with the usual blunt, short and clear prayer of the African children. "Please God", she prayed, "Send us hot water bottle today. It will not be good tomorrow, God, as the baby will dead, so please send it this afternoon." And then she added, "While you are about it, would you please send a dolly for the little girl so that she knows that you really love her?"

The doctor admitted that he was on the spot. As often with children's prayers he felt that he could hardly say Amen. He thought it impossible, but his Christian belief and faith taught him that all things are possible, and God could answer this particular prayer.

Following the prayer session the doctor was teaching in the nurses' training school when he received a message that there was a car at the front door of his home. By the time he reached his house the car had departed but there on the front steps was a 22-pound parcel. He felt tears come to his eyes. He couldn't open the box alone so we called the children at the orphanage to come and help him. Together they pulled off the string and wrapping paper. Excitement was mounting. Some thirty to forty pairs of eyes were focused on the box. From the top layer the doctor lifted out brightly colored knitted jerseys. Then a box of mixed raisins and sultanas - that would make a large batch of cookies for the weekend. Next a supply of much needed medicine and bandages for the sick.

Then, as he put his hand in again, he felt the . . . could it really be? Yes a brand new rubber hot water bottle. Ruth was in the front row watching and when she saw the hot water bottle she rushed forward crying out, "If God has sent the bottle He must have sent the dolly too." Rummaging down to the bottom of the box she pulled out a small beautifully dressed doll. Her eyes gleamed, she had never doubted. Looking up at the doctor she asked, "Can I go with you and give this dolly to that little girl, so she knows God loves her?" "Of course you can," said the doctor and they left immediately to visit with the little girl.

The parcel had been on its way for five whole months, packed by the First Baptist Church in Roanoke, GA. The mission committee had heard and obeyed God's prompting to send a hot water bottle, even to the equator. One of the girls had put in a doll for an African child five months before, in answer to the believing prayer of a 10 year-old to bring it that afternoon. Prayer is one of the best free gifts we receive. There is no cost, but a lot of rewards. Let's continue praying for one another. Heavenly Father, I ask you to bless my friends. Minister to their spirit. Where there is pain give them your peace and mercy. Where there is self-doubting release a renewed confidence to work through them. Where there is tiredness or exhaustion, I ask you to give them understanding, guidance, and strength. Bless their finances, give them greater vision, and raise up friends to support and encourage them. I pray this in the name of Jesus Christ. Amen.

SPELLING PROBLEMS

"Continue the things that you have learned." **2 Timothy 3:14**

My father was cleaning out the house after my mother passed away. It was a place we called home for more than 60 years and although we had grown up and gone off to school, served in the military and begun our own families, the house was still home and contained a treasure of memorabilia from our younger years. Dad wanted to reorganize the place and get rid of the junk. And I couldn't blame him.

As I rummaged through my stuff I discovered something I felt would be instructive for Steve, my son, who was an 11 year-old fifth-grader. It was my Grade 5 Spelling Book. I thought I could show him how much tougher things were when I was in his grade at school. But, when Steve and I later compared his book to mine, we agreed that his words were more difficult.

As I considered this I began to think about the culture in which our children are growing up. It is not just spelling that is harder. Life itself has added layers of demands and is much more difficult and tougher since my school days.

With our changing culture, comes the changing of words and their meaning. There are words and expressions that we don't hear anymore. For example:

- Be sure to refill the **ice trays** we're having company tonight.
- Watch for the **postman.** I need to mail this letter.
- Quit slamming the **screen door** when your go out and come in.

- Don't forget to **win the clock** before you go to bed.
- Roll up your **britches legs** so they don't get caught in the bicycle chain.
- Don't go outside with your **school clothes** on.
- Take that empty bottle to the store so you won't have to **pay a deposit** on the next ones.
- Put a **dish towel** over the cake to keep the flies off.
- Quit jumping on the floor, I have a **cake in the oven.**
- Let me know when the **Fuller Brush man** comes I need a few things.
- There is a dollar in my purse, get **5 gallons of gas** when you go to town.
- Don't lose that **button;** I won't be able to sew it back on.
- Quit **crossing your eyes**! They will get stuck that way.
- Put the bottles out for the **milk man,** and put a note on them for One quart of **heavy cream.**

Several years ago I flew a charter flight for a couple of cattle buyers from Illinois to west Texas. We landed at a small airport and were met by the rancher who was selling the cattle. He drove us to town to a small hotel. The place looked like the set from the movie Gun smoke. When I checked in and went to my room, I noticed a sign on the door. **This room is air conditioned. For best results open the transom and raise the window.** A new meaning for air-conditioning. And so it was.

Times have changed. New words have come into our vocabulary. Cool doesn't relate to temperature and wicked can mean either good or bad. With so much overt sinfulness being pushed into our children it becomes harder and harder for them to resist temptation and do what is right. New negative influences challenge our young people as they try to make wise choices.

Yet the answer is the same as it has always been. "From childhood we have known the Holy Scriptures," that is how Paul characterized Timothy's training, 2 Timothy 3:15. This still the way it should be for our children. No matter how tough the times or the situations they are always spelled out in **God's Word**. It is one book that never changes.

> ***Begin to train them early***
> ***To fear and love the Lord.***
> ***To carry on life's pathway,***
> ***God's lamp. . . .*** *His Holy Word.*

HAVE YOU EVER HAD A DOG

Introduction: Question the group by asking: **Do you have a dog? What is his or her name? Is it a small or large dog? What do you like about your dog?**

Does your dog due tricks? Does your dog know how to speak? Can your dog talk?

I have a story about a dog who could talk. A man was driving through the hills of New Hampshire and saw a sign in front of a broken down farm house. The sign said, **"TALKING DOG FOR SALE."** The man was curious so he stopped and rang the bell. The owner came to the door and when asked if he had a talking dog, replied, "Yep! He is in the back yard."

They went to the back-yard and there sat a beautiful German Dachshund. (Wiener dog) "Do you talk?" asked the man. "YA!" answered the dog.

After the man recovered from the shock of hearing the dog talk, he said, "So what is the story?"

The Dachshund looked up and began: "Well, I came from a litter of sixteen and when I was pretty young I discovered that I could talk. I wanted to help the government so I called the CIA. In no time they had me jetting from country to country, sitting in rooms with world leaders and intelligence people because no one figured I would be eavesdropping. I became one of CIA's most valuable spies. After several years of travel it really worn me out so I decided to come home and settle down.

"I got a job at the airport with the TSA agents and I would wander around the airport, near suspicious travelers and listen to their conversations. I uncovered some incredible dealings. I was awarded several service awards and medals. After that I got married and started my own family. Now I am retired.

The man was utterly amazed. He turned to the farmer and asked, "What do you want for this dog?" "**Ten dollars,**" the farmer replied." "Only Ten Dollars?" The man exclaimed. "Why are you selling him so cheap?"

Because he is a liar, he ain't never did any of that stuff!

Morale: Does God think it is okay to tell lies?
What happens when we lie? We have to tell
more lies to cover-up the first one.
God wants each of us to always tell the truth. We must be honest.
Proverbs 24:26 "An honest answer is like a kiss on the lips."

ANOTHER DOG STORY

While driving through the back woods of Montana a man saw a sign in front of a broken-down shanty farm house. The sign read, **"TALKING DOG FOR SALE."** The man was curious so he stopped and rang the bell. The owner came to the door and when asked if he had a talking dog replied, "Yep! He is in the back yard."

They went to the back-yard and there sat a nice looking Golden Labrador retriever. "Do you talk?" asked the man. "Yep," the dog replied.

After the man recovered from the shock of hearing the dog talk, he said, "So what is the story?" Tell me about how you learned to talk.

The Lab looked up and replied, "Well, I discovered I could talk when I was pretty young. I wanted to help the government so I called the CIA. In no time they had me jetting from country to country, sitting in rooms with world leaders and intelligence people because no one figured I would be eavesdropping. I was one of CIA's most valuable spies. After several years all the travel really worn me out, and I wasn't getting any younger so I decided to come home and settle down."

"I got a job at the airport with TSA as an undercover security agent. I would wander around near suspicious travelers and listen to their conversations and I uncovered some incredible dealings. I was awarded a batch of medals. After that I got married and had a mess of puppies. Now I am retired."

The man was utterly amazed. He turned to the farmer and asked, "What do you want for the dog?" "Ten dollars," the farmer replied.

"Ten dollars?" The man exclaimed. "Why on earth are you selling him so cheap?" "Because he is a liar. He ain't never done those things."

Proverbs speaks clearly of the matter of lying. "Truthful lips endure forever, but a lying tongue is but for a moment. Deceit is in the heart of those who devise evil, but those who plan honesty have joy. No ill befalls the righteous but the wicked are filled with trouble. Lying lips are an abomination to the Lord, but those who act faithfully are his delight." Proverbs 12: 19-22.

We learn quickly that lying requires a lot of skill. Once a lye is perpetrated it requires addi8tinal lies to support it. Each step is support of the first falsehood becomes increasingly more difficult to sustain.

The lips of the righteous know what is acceptable but the mouth of the wicked learn what is perverse." Proverbs 10:32.

LABOR DAY FOR THE LORD

This is **Labor Day** weekend. It is a National legal holiday that was established more than 100 years ago. In 1884 in fact. Over the years it has evolved from a purely **labor union celebration** into a general "last fling of summer" festival. Although it is not a religious holiday per se, we can see it as part of our Christian heritage as we recognize the working class of our nation. It also marks the time that many colleges, secondary and elementary school begin classes. A subtle blessing for all mothers who have endured their kids all summer long.

Labor Day is celebrated on the first Monday of September in the USA. Canada has its own Labor Day holiday. As a spiritual thought we need to share some scripture that will bring bearing to this weekend holiday. The following scripture has application:

> **"W**hat does man gain from all of his labor at which he toils under the sun? Generations come and generations go, but the earth remains forever. The sun rises and the sun sets, and hurries back to where it rises. The wind blows to the south and turns to the north, round and round it goes ever returning on its course. All streams flow into the sea, yet the sea is never full To the place the streams come from, there they will return again. All things are wearisome, more than one can say. The eye never has enough of seeing, nor the ear its fill of hearing. What has been will be again, what has been done will be done again. There is nothing new under the sun. Is there anything of which one would? Say look this is something new. There

is no-remembrance of former things and even of those who are yet to come will not be remembered by those who follow." Ecclesiastes 1:3-11

These words found in Ecclesiastes are thought to have been written by King Solomon with his life largely behind him. He takes stock of the world as he has experienced it, between the horizons of birth and death. The latter horizon beyond which man cannot see. And, in spite of all of King Solomon's wisdom and experience he teaches us that God has ordered all things according to His purposes, and that Man should be patient and enjoy life as God gives it. Man should know his own limitations and not vex himself. He should be prudent in everything, living carefully before God, fearing God and keeping His commandments.

Of course being a Senior Citizen and having experienced various events in our lives we sometimes have a tendency to think that we have all of the answers.

Sometimes we only wished we did. Someone once said, **"Remember, once you get over the hill, you'll begin to pick up speed."**

I heard a cute story the other day, please allow me to share it with you:

Seems an older couple were lying in bed one morning.

They had just awakened from a good night's sleep. He takes her hand and she responds, "Don't touch me. "Why not?" He asked. She answered, "Because I'm dead!"

The husband asked, "What are you talking about?"

We are both lying in bed together, and talking to one another."

She said "No, I'm definitely dead." He insisted, "You are not dead."

"What in the world makes you think you're dead?" He asked.

"Because I woke up this morning and nothing hurts."

Scriptures teaches us that God won't give us more than we can handle. But then there are times when we wish that He didn't trust us quite so much.

King Solomon concludes his writings with this passage from Ecclesiastes:

"Fear God and keep his commandments, for this is the whole duty of man. For God will bring every deed into judgment. Including every hidden thing, whether it is good or evil." Ecclesiastes 12:13 NIV

A Sweet Lesson in Humanity

Several years ago I had the good fortune to return to my home town in Illinois, where I went to high school, and had so many fond memories. It was a thrill to return to the various locations that triggered the happy times of my life.

In the last two years of high school, I worked in a drug store as a soda/lunch counter clerk. I made milk shakes and sundaes, fried hamburgers and grilled cheese sandwiches. It was a great job, I earned a little spending money and I met many people who became my friends through the years. To be able to return to Coe's Drug Store on Fifth and Jefferson Streets in Springfield, Illinois and sit at the counter, drink a Coke and remember the old days was a pleasant experience.

While I was sipping my coke I noticed a young boy come in and sit on the stool next to me. He was very proper and patiently waited for the waitress to take his order. When she arrived, he asked the waitress, "What does an ice cream sundae cost?" "Fifty cents," was the reply.

Fifty cents, I thought. Wow! The price of ice cream has really increased. When I worked there you could get a sundae for 20 cents and add pecans for a nickel. The chocolate syrup and whipped cream topping was included.

The little boy, who probably about 10 years old, reached down into his pocket and pulled out a hand full of coins. He counted the money very carefully but the waitress grew impatient. She had bigger and more important customers to wait on. Finally the little boy said,

"How much would just a plain dish of ice cream be? The waitress responded, with a noticeable irritation in her voice, "Thirty-five cents."

Again the boy counted his money and then said, "May I have some plain vanilla ice cream, in a dish please?" He gave the waitress the correct amount of money and she returned with the ice cream.

Later the waitress returned to clear off the counter and as she picked up the boy's dish she felt a lump in her throat. There on the counter were two nickels and five pennies. She realized that he had enough money for the chocolate sundae with whipped cream and nuts but had sacrificed it so that he could leave her a tip.

The moral of the story: Before passing judgment, first treat others with courtesy, dignity and respect.

The story of the boy's action is a beautiful illustration of an act of humanity. That is having the fact or quality of being humane. He demonstrated what is considered to be the best qualities that a person can have. They include:

- Kindness
- Tenderness
- Mercy and
- Being sympathetic.

Humanity is being the child of God. God wants us to emulate Him. He encourages us to be like Him and imitate His example. Do we d that? Are we overlooking a very simple and basic quality of life?

"There are three things in the game of life that are important: First, Be kind, second, be kind, and third be kind."

THE WORD OF GOD

Blessed is he who **reads** and those who **hear** the words of prophecy, and keep those things which are written in it; for the time is near. All Scripture is given by inspiration of God, and is profitable for doctrine, for reproof, for correction, for instruction in righteousness, that the man of God may be complete, and thoroughly equipped for every good work. The word of God is living and powerful.

The paradox of our time in history and the season in which we live, has to frustrate us;

- We have taller buildings but shorter tempers.
- We have wider Freeways, but narrower viewpoints.
- We spend more money but have less to show for it.
- We buy more but don't enjoy it as much.
- We have bigger homes and smaller families.
- We possess more appliances and conveniences but have less time.
- We have more education and diplomas but less common sense.
- We have more knowledge but less judgment.
- We have more expertise yet more problems.
- We have more medicine but less wellness.

Have we failed to heed the words of the scriptures? Is it because we think we can do it ourselves without the Lord's help? Or is it because we think we have all of the answers?

- We have learned how to make a living but not a life.
- We have added years to life, not life to years.
- We have been all the way to the moon and back but have trouble crossing the street to meet a new neighbor.
- We have cleaned up the air but polluted the soul.
- We have conquered the atom but we can't overcome prejudice.
- We write more but learn less.
- We plan more but accomplish very little.
- We have learned to rush but not to wait.
- These are the days of quick trips; disposable diapers; throwaway morality, and one night stands.
- We are challenged with overweight bodies and pills that do everything from making us thinner or cheering us up to making us sleep.

All scripture is inspired by God. It provides us with answers and solutions to our problems. Remember to spend more time with your loved ones, because they aren't going to be around forever. Give a warm hug to the one next to you, it's a treasure you can give from your heart that doesn't cost a cent. Hold hands for it is the personal touch that will be cherished by the person who may not be there again. Say I love you to your loved ones, and mean it. Share a kind word with someone who looks up to you. Remember that life has a way of moving quickly and catching us unaware of the passing years.

Life goes by quickly. It seems to accelerate as it gets closer to the end. So do what you can today as you can never be certain whether this is your season or not. Life is a gift. The way we live our lives is a blessing to those who follow. Make it a fantastic one.

Knowing and living **God's Word** is powerful and rewarding. The blessing is yours.

Do Not Worry About Life

Do you worry about life? Does worry get you down? What causes your anxiety? What does Jesus say about worry?

> *"Therefore I tell you, do **not worry** about your life, what you will eat or about your body, what you will wear. Life is more than food and the body more than clothes. Consider the ravens; they do not sow or reap, they have no store room or barn; yet God feeds them. And how much more valuable you are than the birds! Who of you by worrying can add a single hour to your life? Since you cannot do this very little thing, why do you worry?" Luke 12: 22-24 NIV*

A young lady was worrying and complaining to her father about how difficult her life had become. No matter what she did, she said, "It never seemed to work out right. Everything I try to do goes wrong. Each time I make plans they never turn out right. I don't know what to do."

The father didn't say anything. He thought he had the answer. He had an illustration that he thought may help his daughter to understand. He simply took her to the kitchen and put three pans of water on the stove. He carefully adjusted the heat on each pan. As the pans began to boil he added something to each pan. To the first pan he added carrots, to the second pan he added two eggs, and to the third pan he put in some coffee grounds.

After all three pans had cooked a while he put their contents into separate bowls and asked his daughter to follow his directions.

He said, "From the first pan cut the carrots into bite size pieces". When his daughter had done this, he told her, "Now cut the eggs into pieces." Finally, he instructed his daughter to smell and taste the coffee. "Okay," said his daughter, rather impatiently, "What does all this mean?" She simply could not understand the lesson.

"Each food," the father said, "Teaches us something about adversity and why we need not worry. The carrots went into the boiling water **hard** but came out **soft and weak**. The eggs went in **soft and fragile** but came out hardened. The coffee, however. Changed the water to something better."

"Which of these three items will you be like as you face life? Will you give up and become **soft** like the **carrots**, or will you become **hard** as the eggs? Will you **not worry** and simply let God transform adversity into triumph? As had happened with the coffee. You are the chef of your own life, what will you bring to the table?"

Although it seems difficult and almost impossible sometimes, what we must to do is let God do the worrying and trust that He will help us make the right decisions.

An Oath of Miracles

A little girl by the name of Tess went to her bedroom and pulled a glass jelly jar from its hiding place in the closet. The jar contained a number of coins that she had been saving. She carefully poured the change out on her bed and began to count it. She counted the money three times because she had to be absolutely certain how much she had. It had to be perfect, no chance for a mistake.

She carefully placed the coins back into the jar, twisting the cap on tight. She slipped out the back door and made her way to the Rite Aid Drug Store n Post Road. She went directly to the chief pharmacist and waited patiently for him to give her some attention. He seemed to be very busy so Tess twisted her feet and made scuffling noises to let him know she was waiting. But, nothing she seemed to do worked. She cleared her throat several times with a disgusting sound, hoping it would get his attention. Finally she took a quarter from the jar and banged it on the glass. That worked.

"So what do you want?" Asked the pharmacist in an annoyed tone of voice. "Can't you see that I am talking with my brother from Chicago, whom I haven't seen in ages?" he added.

"Well, I want to talk to you about my brother," Tess said. "He is very, very sick and I want to buy a miracle. His name is Andrew and he has something bad growing in his head. How much does a miracle cost?" Asked Tess.

"We don't sell miracles," the pharmacist replied. "I am sorry, but I can't help you."

"But listen, I have money to pay for it," pleaded Tess. "My father said that only a miracle can save him now. I have some money and if it isn't enough I will get more. Just tell how much it will be?"

The well-dressed man with whom the pharmacist had been talking, stooped down and ask the little girl, "What kind of miracle does your brother need?" I don't know," answered Tess, with her eyes beginning to well-up, "I just know he is very sick and Mommy says he must have an operation. But my Daddy can't pay for it. So I want to use my money." "How much do you have" asked the well-dress man from Chicago. "One dollar and eleven cents," was the reply. "And it is all the money I have, but I can get more if I need to," said Tess.

"Well, what a coincidence, a dollar and eleven cents is exactly the price of a miracle for your little brother, said the man. He took her money in one hand and grasped Tess's finger with the other. "Take me to where you live, I want to meet your brother and talk with your parents. Let's see if I have the miracle you need."

The pharmacist's brother, the well-dressed man from Chicago was **Dr. Carlton Armstrong,** a famous surgeon specializing in neuro-surgery. The operation was scheduled and subsequently completed, free of charge. It wasn't long before Andrew was at home again doing well.

Mom and Dad were happily asking about the chain of events that led them to this place. "That surgery was a real miracle, I wonder how much it cost?" the mother asked. One dollar and eleven cents plus the faith of a little girl. In our lives we never know how many miracles we will need. A miracle is not suspension of natural **law,** but the gift of a **higher law** from God.

FRIENDSHIP

A ball is a circle, it is round without end.
It keeps us together like the circle of friends.
But the treasure inside for you to see, is the treasure
Of friendship you've granted to me.
Today I pass the friendship ball to you.

My oath when you're sad will dry your tears.
When frightened, will comfort your fears.
When you are worried, will give you faith and hope,
If you're confused will help you cope.
When you are lost, and can't see the light,
I'll be your beacon shinning so bright.
This my oath, my pledge to the end,
Why, you may ask? Because you are my friend.
God loves you always.
Anonymous

SERVING THE LIVING GOD

Hebrews 9: 14 "How much more then will the blood of Christ, who through the Holy Spirit offered himself, unblemished, to God, cleanse our conscience from acts that Lead to death, so that we may serve the Living God."

Grandpa was 90 some years of age. He sat feebly on the piano bench. He didn't move, he simply sat there quietly with his head down, staring at his hands. His young grand-daughter, Stacey, sat down next to him. He didn't acknowledge her presence and the longer she sat there she began to wonder if he was okay.

Finally, not really wanting to disturb him, but wanting to check on him, she asked, "Grandpa are you alright?" He raised his head and looked at her, smiled, and said in a strong clear voice, "Yes, I am fine. Thank you for asking."

Stacey replied, "I didn't mean to disturb you Grandpa, but you were just sitting here staring at your hands." Her grandpa smiled and asked, "Have you really ever looked at your hands?" Stacey opened her hands and stared down at them. She turned them over and she looked at the tops of her hands then turned them over again and looked at the palms. She couldn't figure out the point that he was making.

Grandpa winked, and began this story: "Stop and think for a moment about the hands that you have; how they serve you so well. These hands of mine, though wrinkled and worn, shriveled and weak, have been the tools that I have used for many years. They have reached out and embraced life. They put food in my mouth and clothes on my back

- As a child, my mother taught me to fold them in prayer.
- They tied my shoes, buttoned my buttons and pulled on my coat.
- They have been dirty and clean, scraped and raw, blistered and bent.
- They were particularly clumsy when I tried to hold my first born baby.
- Adorned with my wedding ring they showed the world that I was married
- And loved someone special.
- They trembled and shook when I buried my mother and father.
- They were rung in grief when I lost my wife.
- They held my daughter's hand as she walked down the aisle at her wedding.
- They have covered my face, combed my hair, shaved my chin and brushed my teeth.
- They have cleansed the rest of my body.
- They have been sticky and wet, broken and raw.
- To this day, when nothing else of me works well, they hold me up, lay me down and continue to fold in prayer.
- These hands are the mark of where I have been and represent the ruggedness of my life.
- But, more importantly it will be these hands that God will reach for and take when he leads me home.
- And with these hands He will lift me to His side and there I will reach out and touch the face of Jesus Christ.

When our hands are tired and sore we need to think of what Stacey's Grand-father said and know that we too will be stroked and caressed by the hand of God. We need to know and watch for the answer to prayer and how it continues to work in our committed lives. Let's continue praying for one another, serving the Living God.

IT IS TOUGH TO BRING
A HELLCAT DOWN

After reading a story entitled **Fast, Cheap and Out of Control,** by Peter Merlin, I was reminded of a similar flight of a Grumman F6F Hellcat from Chincoteague, Va. In 1956. Utility Squadron Four, VU-4, operated from NAS Chincoteague, Va. (Now known as Wallops Island, NASA.) VU-4's mission was to provide flights for Navy ships operating off the mid-Atlantic coast, conducting CIC (Combat Information Center) Radar training, and Radar Controlled Anti-Aircraft Fire support. First came the radar vectoring, followed by a target sleeve towed by an airplane, and finally a real live shoot-out using a full sized, WWII fighter made by Grumman Aircraft.

More than 12,000 F6F Hellcats were built between 1942 and 1945. It was one of the most successful fighters flown by the Navy. It was simple, rugged and could take a great deal of punishment. Making the Hellcat into a drone airplane in the early 50's was a good idea. Just paint the airplane red, install a remote controlled auto pilot and it became a perfect flying target. After ten hours of proving flights with a safety pilot on board the drone was ready to serve the mission as a NOLO, No Live Pilot On Board target.

Flying a chase airplane, known as "Charlie" on a drone shoot was exciting and almost like being engaged in actual combat. The squadron was very experienced in drone shoots, operating one airplane that had survived 25 missions, returning home with gaping holes and flak damage, but still flying.

On one particular day the drone shoot became a memorable event. The F6F was preflight, ground checked and put into the launch position. Charlie 1, 2 and 3, the primary control chase planes came swooping down to pick up the airplane as Fox", the ground controller, added power for the takeoff. All went well and it was a picture book launch. The Hellcat climbed like a home sick angel. The group was on its way to rendezvous with a ship located in Warning Area 387A about 150 miles east of Cape Charles. Virginia.

Climb out appeared to be routine until Charlie 1 reported that he could not get the airplane to respond to his inputs. Charlie 2 and then Charlie 3 tried without success. The airplane was climbing with climb power and it continued until it reached its service ceiling, about 13,500 feet. As it leveled off it began a lazy turn to the left. It was almost as though the airplane was saying, "I'm happy right here boys, I'm not going anywhere with you."

Lt. Steinbring, Charlie 1, called base operations on his radio and reported the difficulty. The Operations Duty Officer went through a check list of items to try to correct the problem. No luck. Finally, the OPS Officer ordered the group to shoot the drone down. The F8F Bearcats, flown by the chase pilots, were armed with twin 50 caliber machine guns. The Hellcat was a sitting duck. What a break to shoot down one of your own airplanes.

Charlie 1, then Charlie 2 and finally Charlie 3 made numerous runs on the drone. They could not shoot it down. In fact, they used up all of their ammunition. In desperation they reported the situation to Base Operations. After a conference with Captain White, the commanding officer of VU-4, a decision was made to call the Air Force to see if they could destroy the drone.

Can you imagine what went through the mind of the Operations Officer at Langley Air Force Base at Newport News, Va. when he received this call? Unbelievable! The Air Force is going to shoot down a Navy fighter. A dream come true. Unfortunately, the Duty Officer did not have the authority to launch any fighters to intercept the drone. He had to get orders from Washington. He was on the phone in a flash.

Meanwhile, the drone continued to make circles at 13,000 feet and the prevailing westerly winds were blowing it further and further out to sea. Lt. Steinbring decided to try his auto pilot control again, and eureka, the drone responded. By now the group had used up a lot fuel and it was determined that it would be unwise to try and get it back home to NAS Chincoteague.

The decision was to ditch the airplane in the sea. Lt. Cunningham, Charlie 2 had always wondered what it would be like to make an emergency landing at sea. He took control and remotely flew the airplane down to the surface, extended the wing flaps and with the landing gear still up, landed the airplane in a swell. The landing was perfect. After the splash down the airplane seemed to bob to the surface and began to float. Lt. Cunningham reported later that **if** he had been on board he would have had time to get out of his harness, inflate the raft, and climb into it without even getting his feet wet. Now the airplane became a hazard to surface vessels. What can be done? After about twelve minutes the F6Fslowlysank below the surface. A final tribute to a tough, rugged fighter that didn't give up easily. **It is tough to bring a Hellcat down.**

Al Schmid

USNR   575719

CONCRETE LOVE

"You will find as you look back on your life, the moments when you Have really lived are the moments when you have done things in the Spirit of love." *Henry Drummond*

Several years ago, my pastor's wife told a story about her husband who had spent many hours building a new driveway at their home. He had carefully leveled the ground, moved the extra dirt by wheelbarrow loads to the back yard. He had staked the forms, and raked in pea-stone gravel to make a solid base. The concrete-mixer truck came, poured the fresh concrete into the forms and he carefully smoothed the surface to make it look like a professional job.

Just has he finished the job, two of his small children chased a ball across the driveway leaving deep footprints in the fresh concrete. Charlie, being a preacher and not apt to use "blue words," yelled after the kids with a torrent of angry indignation. He shocked his wife who responded by saying, "You are a minister who is supposed to **love children,** and that was not a very good example."

Fuming, Charlie shouted, ***"I love children in the abstract, not in the concrete."*** The alleged incident was a humorous play on words, but the story rings true. If we agree with the concept and fail to adhere to the principle, that of self-giving love, we have fallen short. How often do we neglect to express our love to the people we live and work with each day?

The Bible describes Christian love in terms of its tangible expression: "Love suffers long and is kind; love does not envy; love does not parade itself, it is not puffed up, does not behave rudely, and

126

does not seek its own is not provoked, thinks no evil." (11 Corinthians 13: 4-5).

As a **theory,** love isn't worth much. As a **practice,** it is the world's greatest treasure. When the footprints are in the driveway, people discover whether their love exists in the abstract or in the concrete.

Oscar Hammerstein, the beloved composer and playwright, after learning he had cancer, went to Mary Martin's dressing room during the performance of **Sound of Music** and added these words to her famous song:

> "A Bell is no bell till you ring it.
> A song is no song till you sing it.
> The love in your heart wasn't put there to stay.
> For love isn't love till you give it away."

1 John 4: 7 says. *"Beloved, let us love one another, for love is of God."*

A teacher was lecturing to his class and asked the students this question:

"How can we know when the darkness is leaving and the dawn is coming?

The students were puzzled and after a while they asked for the answer. The teacher replied, "We know the darkness is leaving when we can see another person and know that he is our brother or sister; otherwise no matter what time it is, it is still dark." "Love is the light of the world." The richest source of healing is to know the darkness is leaving when we see the light and when we give ourselves in love.

Love is the mark of a believer, and people who share their love are recognized as belonging to Christ. God longs to fill our hearts with love, and He expects us to share that love with others.

> *Follow with reverent steps, the great example...*
> *Of Him whose holy work was doing good;*
> *So shall the wide earth seem our Father's Temple?*
> *Each loving life, a psalm of gratitude. --- Whittier*

Happines Depends On Your Preception

Jesus was an itinerant preacher. After he chose his disciples he went throughout Galilee teaching in the synagogues, preaching the good news of the kingdom, and healing every disease and sickness among the people. News of his miracles spread all over Syria. People brought to him those who were ill with various diseases, people who were suffering severe pain, those having seizures, and were paralyzed, many who were demon possessed. Jesus healed them. He healed them all. Large crowds from Galilee, the Decapolis, Jerusalem, Judea, and the region across the Jordan heard of Jesus' miracles and they came to follow him.

Now when Jesus saw the crowds he went up on a mountain and sat down with the disciples. As the people began to gather around him he began to teach them saying:

> *"Blessed are the poor in spirit for theirs*
> *is the kingdom of heaven.*
> *Blessed are those who mourn for they will be comforted,*
> *Blessed are the meek for they will inherit the earth.*
> *Blessed are those who hunger and thirst for*
> *righteousness for they will be filled.*
> *Blessed are the merciful for they will be shown mercy.*
> *Blessed are the pure in heart for they will see God.*
> *Blessed are the peacemakers, for they*
> *will be called sons of God.*

Blessed are those who are persecuted because of
righteousness for theirs is the kingdom of heaven.
Blessed are you when people insult you, persecute you
and say all kinds of things against you because of m
Rejoice and be glad, because great is your reward
in heaven. For in the same way they persecuted the
*prophets who were before you." **Matthew 5: 3-12 NIV***

You undoubtedly recognize the sermon Jesus gave on the mountain, it contains the Beatitudes. It is often referred to as the **Sermon on the Mount**. Jesus uses the word **blessed** which is defined as: *"Enjoying great happiness or comfort of Joy."* It is a strong message with the promise of happiness, if we choose to accept it. But it also depends on how we perceive it. How do we grasp it, or become mentally aware of it? Perhaps this story may help us to understand.

A man pulled into a gas station on the outskirts of an attractive suburban town to buy gasoline. He had been traveling some distance and his tank was nearly empty. As he filled the tank, he remarked to the attendant, "I have just accepted a new job in this town. I have never been to this part of the country. What are the people like here?"

"What are the people like where you came from?" the attendant asked. "Not so nice," replied the man. "In fact they aren't pleasant at all, they can be quite rude. I do not regret making this move."

The attendant shook his head. "Well, I'm afraid you will find the people in this town to be the same way." Just then another car pulled into the station and stopped at the next pump. "Excuse me," the driver called out. "I am just moving to this area. What can you tell me about it? It certainly is attractive. Is it nice here?"

"Was it nice where you came from?" the attendant asked. "Oh, yes! I come from a great place. The people there are very friendly and I hate to leave. But, I am looking forward to meeting new people and making new friends."

"Well, you'll find the same to be true of this town."

"So what is this town really like?" asked the first man, who had now become irritated with the attendant's conflicting answers.

The attendant just shrugged his shoulders and said, "It's all a matter of perception. **You will find things to be the way you think they are."**

Paul Harvey, radio commentator, once said, "I have never seen a monument erected to a pessimist." Believing is a positive emotion and we must have positive thoughts. **Change your thoughts and you change the world."**

JUST BELIEVE

A man was driving through the country side one afternoon on his way to an important church meeting. The road was curving and it went up and down steep hills. He glanced at his watch and decided that he would arrive on time provided he didn't get lost. As he tried to read the road map, to check his progress, he accidently drove off the road and ended up in a ditch. Although he wasn't injured and the car didn't seem to be damaged it was obvious that he was stuck deep in the mud. No point in trying to call Triple-A so the man walked to the nearest farm to ask for help.

A farmer came to the door and when the man asked if he could get some help getting his car out of the muddy ditch the farmer said, "Sure, Winston can get you out of that ditch," and he pointed to an old mule standing in the paddock down at the barn. The man looked at the tired, old, haggard mule and then back at the farmer who just stood there repeating, "Yep, old Winston can do the job." The man figured he had nothing to lose so he told the farmer to give it a try. The two men and Winston made their way back to the car.

The farmer hitched the mule to the back of the car. With a snap of the reins he shouted "Pull Jake, pull Fred, and pull Ted! Pull Winston! And the mule pulled the car from the ditch with very little effort.

The man was amazed. He thanked the farmer, patted Winston on the head and started to turn to leave. "Excuse me sir," the man said to the farmer, "Why did you call out all those other names before you called on Winston?" The farmer grinned and replied, "Old Winston is just about blind, he can't see anything, and he doesn't hear too well

131

either. As long as he believes he's part of a team, he doesn't mind pulling."

"There are two ways of exerting one's strength; one is pushing down, the other is pulling up." Booker T. Washington (1856-1915)
"Nobody will believe in you unless you believe in yourself." Liberace (1919-1987)

In the Old Testament, 2 Chronicles chapter 9, we read about the Queen of Sheba going to visit Solomon. The Queen had heard of Solomon's fame and she went to Jerusalem to test him with some hard questions. When she met with Solomon she talked with him about all she had on her mind. Solomon answered all of her questions; nothing seemed to be too hard for him to explain to her. The Bible says that the Queen of Sheba was impressed, she saw the Wisdom of Solomon, as well as the palace he had built and all of his wealth and possessions. She was overwhelmed. She said to Solomon, "The report I heard in my own country about your achievements and your wisdom is true. But I did not believe what they said until I came and saw it with my own eyes.

Someone once said, **"Hearing informs and enlightens, but seeing is believing."**

In James the first chapter we read these words:

"....whenever you face trials of many kinds,
you know that the testing of
Your faith develops perseverance.
Perseverance must finish its work so
That you may be mature and complete,
not lacking anything. If any of
You lacks wisdom, he should ask God who
gives generously to all with-
Out finding fault, and it will be given to
him. But when he asks he must
Believe and not doubt, because he who
doubts is like a wave of the sea.

WANTS AND NEEDS

When my children were young, I would often quietly ease-drop on their nighttime prayers before going to bed. After they had gotten through all of their "God bless" prayers they would sometimes switch to their lists of "**wants**". Lord, I **want** to be able to run faster; I **want** to get an "A" on my biology exam; I **want** a new baseball glove; and so on. Their motives were usually innocent in that they didn't consciously distinguish between material things and spiritual things.

As a concerned parent I felt obligated to teach them the difference between *wants and needs.* Ironically, our Adult Sunday School class had a lesson on that very subject. The scripture used was in **James 4: Verse 3**, particularly applicable; *"**When you ask, you do not receive, because you ask with wrong motives, that you may spend on what you get on your pleasures.**"*

James 4: 1-5 NIV offers a clear and succinct explanation.

One of the simplest rules of life is to know the difference between **wants and needs.** In today's society we are constantly challenged by having to make a choice as to whether we truly **need** something, or do we merely **want** it? We are bombarded by the media, pampered by advertising, and coerced by TV, all of whom would like us to believe that we really need the product or the service. We just can't live without it. All of our friends have one or are getting it. The question is: "Do we really **NEED it**?"

How do we define **NEEDS** and **WANTS**? Someone once said that WANT is the "Mistress of Invention and the Devil of debt." Many go through life struggling financially because they cannot discern the difference between their **wants** and their **needs**. NEEDS on one hand are compelled by necessity, or something that cannot be done without. Paul's letter to the Church at Philippi, says: *"**And my God will meet all of your needs, according to His glorious riches in Christ Jesus.**"* Ch. 4:19. NIV

As an adult, I now critique my prayer requests to be certain that I'm asking for the right thing, and for the right reason. When I **want** something, I ask myself, if I can't do without? Is it something that I desire that will further God's kingdom? God will see to it that all my needs are met, and any "wants" are simply a bonus.

The most important requests we can make are spiritual things of God. Such as:

- Peace - not a passive but an active virtue.
- Patience - a gift that God gives only to those He loves.
- Wisdom - knowing what to do next.
- Guidance through God's guardianship.

When we are filled with the goodness of God, the rest will either come in God's time, or it really doesn't matter. God knows even better than we do what is truly needed. We need to strengthen our faith and allow God to guide us and lead us in our choices. He will keep our priorities in order and provide that which we need.

Lord: We know that we fail you when our priorities are not in order. Sometimes we ask for things that aren't always in our best interest. Help us to ask for those things that will glorify you and will Further our spiritual life with you. Amen.

ANSWERING A PAGE

We had just gone through the airport security check with TSA prior to boarding our commercial flight back to Providence. The trip had been very successful and we were anxious to get home. It is always more comfortable to sleep in your own bed than the big king-size ones in the luxury hotel where we stayed.

As we approached our loading gate I thought that I heard my name being called over the airport paging system. "Paging Mr. Al Schmid, Paging Mr. Al Schmid." Now what is this all about? Maybe the flight has been delayed or cancelled? Maybe there is a problem with our baggage? Maybe the flight was oversold and we won't be able to get on board? I thought for a minute and then remembered that I had a small Swiss Army knife in my pocket when I went through security. I really didn't think it would be challenged. It only had a 1/2 " blade but security felt it was a threat and I was asked to forfeit the weapon. I had a choice, either give them the knife, or go to another desk, put the knife in a shipping container and mail it home. Total cost would be $12.75. A new knife would cost me $6.00. Not a tough decision. I told them they could keep the knife.

Was that the reason I was being paged? Did the FBI or CIA want to interrogate me? In any event, I checked with an airline agent, who told me, "Pick up a red phone, give your name, and ask why you was being paged." I found a red phone, picked it up and called, but the operator said, "No we didn't page you." But, I insisted, I had heard the page and it was my name. The operator said, "I am sorry sir, but we never paged you." I never found out what had happened.

On the flight home I recalled the story of a young boy named Samuel, in the Bible, who heard his name being called. (1 Samuel 3:4) "Then the Lord called him." Samuel answered but he didn't know who was calling. 'Here I am' said Samuel. The scriptures say that Samuel did not know the Lord, nor was the word of the Lord revealed to him. So the temple priest **Eli** had to help him understand who was calling him. It was God who revealed His plan for Samuel's life.

The Lord has a plan for us as well, and He calls to our **hearts.** "Come to me, all of you who labor and are heavy laden, and I will give you rest." (Matt. 11:28) That is His call to us to receive the gift of His salvation, rest, and peace. The Savior is calling us to come to Him.

Jesus calls me---- I must follow.
Follow Him today.
When His tender voice is pleading,
How can I delay?

Christ calls the restless ones to find their rest in Him.

WHY DO WE PRAY

I completed my term of service in the Navy, in the late '50s, and returned with my wife and two small children, to our roots in Springfield, Illinois. It was good to be back home after five years of service. We recognized the importance of finding a church home so we went back to South Side Christian, where we were charter members.

One Sunday at a fellowship dinner, which was held monthly, after the morning worship hour, one of the men of the church came to me and asked if I would lead the group in prayer. **I didn't know what to say.** I told him that my prayers had been limited to the times when the engines began to run rough or the thunderstorms were cracking outside the cockpit window, or the ice was forming on the wings. But, I asked the Lord to provide me with the words and I agreed to lead the members in prayer. And it worked! How many times have you faced a similar situation? Don't you wish that you had a way to offer a beautiful and eloquent prayer with little or no notice?

The average person thinks that praying means kneeling down and saying a few perfunctory, routine or superficial words. Prayer is more than that. It is one of the greatest skills in the world. It can be made beautifully simple and effective, but as with any skill, we must learn the formula and step by step open the circuit to receive the power. Prayer is talking with God. When we have a good friend we talk to that person about a lot of different things. That is part of being a good friend. In the same way we should talk to God about what is happening in our life. God wants us to share our life with him, to tell him about what makes us happy, what makes us sad, what frightens us. He wants to know what we want and what we would like him to do for us and for others we **know** and for whom we have concerns.

Consider these steps to develop your prayer life:

- *Talk to the Lord in simple, everyday language.* Talk to God about everything that is on your mind. And in your heart.
- *Tell God what you want.* Tell him that you want to have him provide you and if he thinks it would be good for you. Let God know that you will accept his decision as to what is best for you and for others.
- *Practice praying during the day.* Somehow we have gotten the idea that we should talk to God only a night, before we go to bed. We can talk with him at any time, even as we drive our car, or wait for the bus, or wait in a doctor's office, or where ever we are. If you have a friend you would talk with them. Then talk with God as you would with your friend.
- *Realize that words are not always necessary when you pray.* Just know that God loves you and he is always there to listen and to observe.
- *Try helping others with your prayers.* Pray not only for your family and your loved ones but also pray for people you do not like or have treated you badly. Choose someone who may be a problem to you and pray for them. Surround them with good will and faith. You will be amazed by the results.
- *Do not put all of your prayers in the form of asking.* Let your prayer consist of all the wonderful things that have happened to you. Name them one by one. Thank God for him hearing and answering your prayers. **Finally,** consider this technique in praying:

AMAZING GRACE

by John Newton 1748

One of the most recognized Christian hymns in the English speaking world is **Amazing Grace,**

Written by an English poet, an Anglican clergyman named John Newton, 1725-1807. The words were published in 1779. The hymn describes, in first person, the move of a "wretch" from lost to found, by a merciful act of God.

It is estimated that **Amazing Grace is** performed about 10 million times a year. The hymn stands as an emblematic African-American spiritual. In the 19th century the hymn was sung by Native Americans enduring the Trail of Tears, by abolitionists, by soldiers of the Civil War, and by homesteaders settling in the prairie territories. It was a hymn that was used during the American Civil Rights movement. Today it has attained tremendous popularity. **Amazing Grace** is John Newton's spiritual autobiography in verse.

In 1725 John Newton was born in Warping, a district in London near the Thames River. His father was a shipping merchant who was brought up Catholic but had Protestant sympathies. His mother was an independent, but unaffiliated with the Anglican Church of England. She intended to have her son John become a clergyman. Unfortunately, she fell sick with tuberculosis and died when John was 6 years old. For the next several years Newton was raised by his emotionally distraught step-mother. Newton became difficult to handle so he was sent to a boarding school where he was considered incorrigible. At the age of eleven he joined his father in the shipping business. He sailed on a number of different vessels as a seaman-apprentice. His career was marbled by headstrong disobedience. His pattern of life came close to death on several occasions. His actions examined a relationship with God but would relapse with his bad behavior.

Finally, Newton joined the Royal Navy but his acts of disobedience continued. He had a series of disagreements with many of this shipmates and he developed a reputation for being one of the most profane men on the ship. His tour in the Royal Navy ended abruptly.

Newton's life changed when he married his wife, Polly. But, he continued his sea going career. In 1750 he was named Captain of a cargo ship that was engaged in transporting slaves from Africa to North America, and it was during one of these voyages that he wrote the lyrics to **Amazing Grace.** The ship he was sailing, named the Greyhound was bound from America to the British Isles when it encounter a fierce North Atlantic storm. During that storm Newton saved the ship and its crew, and also found the Lord. Newton pondered the divine challenge and elected to leave the sailing business and purse a religious education and Theology. His learning's leaned toward evangelism and he began to socialize with the Methodists, and the Bishop of Lincoln. He was ordained and offered the curacy of Olney, Buckinghamshire, in 1764. He lived and worked in the vicarage in Olney until his death in 1807.

A Retiree's Last Trip to Allie's Feed Store

Yesterday I stopped at Allie's Feed store in North Kingstown to pick up a bag of Blue Seal dog food for my pet dog Fenway. Fenway is a miniature, short haired, Dachshund who weighs in at about 15 pounds. He speaks neither German nor English but is able to clearly communicate with us, especially when he is hungry.

I was in the checkout line when a woman behind me asked if I had a dog. What did she think I had? I told her I was starting the Blue Seal diet again. I added that I probably shouldn't because the last time I was on it I ended up in the hospital. I had lost 50 pounds but I ended up in the intensive care ward with tubes coming out of my orifices and an IV in both arms.

I told her that essentially it was a perfect diet and the way it works is to load your jacket pockets with Blue Seal nuggets and simply eat one or two every time you feel hungry. The food is nutritionally complete so it works well and I was going to try it again. (I must mention here that practically everyone in the line was now enthralled with my story.)

Horrified, the lady asked, "If you ended up in the hospital was it because the dog food poisoned you?" I told her no, I stopped to pee on a fire hydrant and a car hit me.

I though the guy behind her was going to have a heart attack, he was laughing so hard,

Allie's said it okay to stop by any time, just be careful what you talk about. Older folks have all the time in the world to think up crazy things to say.

141

DON'T WAIT FOR THE
PREFECT CONDITION

"HE WHO OBSERVES THE WIND WILL NOT SOW." Ecclesiastes. 11: 4 (NIV)

How often do we find ourselves standing at the airport gate, waiting for the airplane to be in place with the jet way perfectly positioned, the weather just right, the provisions stored aboard, the luggage loaded and the flight crew ready to make the boarding announcement? We are anxious to get underway to our planned destination. We are willing to launch out but we are dependent on someone else to complete the pre-flight and finish all of the preparations. All conditions may not always go as planned, but dreams do move forward. Our problem is we often become a little restless waiting for them to happen.

We may look out at the graying clouds or the rain that has started. Our baggage handlers don't seem to be loading the luggage as quickly as they should. The cabin attendants are just standing around talking about their last weekend in Florida, and the gate attendants seem to lack any sense of urgency. What a way to run an airline!

It is time to **stop** waiting for perfection, inspirations, permission to act, reassurance that it is going to work,, someone to change, the right person to come along, the new administration to take over, an absence of risk, a clear set of instructions, more confidence, or even for the pain to go away.

Instead of saying I can't do that, or I don't have the resources, we need to know that "**necessity fuels invention.**" Instead of saying

I've never tried that before we need to say, let's give it a try. Instead of saying it will never get any better, we need to try it one more time. Instead of saying let someone else deal with it, we need to be ready to learn something new. Instead of saying, "It's not my job," say, "I'll be glad to take the responsibility." Instead of saying, "I can't," say, **"By God's grace I can."**

When I was a lad my father asked me to prepare the yard behind the house for a new lawn. It was in the fall. The yard had suffered terribly from a very hot and dry summer. It needed to be cultivated, racked and made ready for seeding. I worked at the task for several days thinking it would never be completed. Finally, it came time for planting. But it was a windy, stormy day and I didn't think it wise to continue with the job.

I was reminded of the scripture: ***"Whoever watches the wind will not plant; whoever looks at the clouds will not reap."* Ecclesiastes 11:4.** I might add, ***"Whoever sees black clouds in the sky will not fly."*** When dad came home from work that night he was not happy with my decision not to plant the seeds. He reminded me of the scripture: ***"Sow your seed in the morning, and at evening let your hands be idle, for you do not know which will succeed, whether this or that, or whether both will do equally well."* Ecclesiastes 11:6.**

For us to accomplish a task or to complete a project we cannot spend all of our time thinking about what must be done. Instead we need to reflect on what we have already accomplished and what we have learned from the results. Football coach John Wooden said, **"Things turn out best, for the people who make the best of the way things turn out."**

There is a strong relationship between our movement toward our dreams and the resources we need becoming available to us. Too often we want to be able to see the resources or even have them in hand before we start moving forward. When we do this we have neither the resource nor the movement.

We need to be like the snail that began climbing up an apple tree one cold wintery day. As he inched his way upward a worm stuck its head out of a crevice in the tree and said, "You are wasting your energy. There isn't a single apple on this tree." The snail kept on climbing and replied, "No, but there will be by the time I get there!" Over and over in the Scriptures God sends his people out with what seems to be little or no resources. But when they got to where God wanted them to be, the resources needed to get the job done were in place, waiting for them. Vision does not follow resources, it happens the other way around. First we have a dream, then we have to move toward it, and the resources follow.

A wise man once said, "Effort only releases its reward after a person refuses to quit." People who succeed see what other people don't and continue to preserver.

WALKING AWAY TIME

The time for "walking away" comes to each of us at some time or another. Maybe it is a **new job, a move to a new community, a marriage, a death, a divorce, a young person leaving home, a son or daughter going off to college, or joining the military.** These are just a few examples of the walk-away experience. They can be emotionally wrenching and extremely stressful. Tough for us and for our loved ones, but they can also be a blessed event.

The children of Israel walked away from everything when Moses led them out of the land of Egypt. Life was difficult in Egypt under the rule of the Pharaoh, but it was familiar. Life was tough but somewhat predictable. Nevertheless, the people heeded God's word, believed in His promises and followed Moses. *"My Presence will go with you, and I will give you rest."* said God. Ex 33:14

During our "walking-away times," our stability and peace of mind comes from the presences of the Lord. God walks with us, He is our forever anchor and we can walk into the future with confidence. What we must do is never forget Him.

> *"Lift up my eyes to the hills—where*
> *does my help come from?*
> *My help comes from the Lord, the*
> *Maker of heaven and earth.*
> *He will not let your foot slip—he who*
> *watches over you will not*
> *Slumber. Indeed, he who watches over*
> *Israel will neither slumber*

> *Nor sleep. The Lord watches over you—*
> *the Lord is your shade and*
> *Your right hand. The sun will not*
> *harm you by day, nor the moon*
> *By night. The Lord will keep you from*
> *all harm—He will watch*
> *Over your life. The Lord will watch over*
> *your coming and going both*
> *Now and forevermore."* Psalm 121:122 NIV

A story about a little boy whose unselfish act demonstrates that God is here and among us. The story illustrates another walking-away experience which ends with a blessing. Bobby, wanted to meet God. He knew that it was a long way to where God lived so he decided to pack a lunch for the trip. He put a bag of potato chips and a six pack of Coca-Cola in his knap-sack and started his journey. When he gone about three blocks he met an old woman who was sitting on a bench in the Park, staring at some pigeons. Bobby sat down next to her and opened his lunch sack. He was about to take a drink of Coke when he noticed the lady looked hungry, so he offered her some of his chips. She smiled and gratefully accepted them. Her smile was pretty and the Bobby wanted to see it again. So he offered her a Coke. She smiled and took it. They sat all afternoon eating and smiling, **but never said a word.**

As twilight approached Bobby realized how tired he was and he got up to leave. Before he had gone more than a few steps he turned back to the woman and gave her a big hug and she gave him her biggest smile.

When the little boy returned home his mother was surprised by the look of joy on his face. "What did you do today that made you so happy?" she asked. Bobby answered, **"I had lunch with God. . . Do you know what? She's got the most beautiful smile I have ever seen!"**

Meanwhile, the old woman, also radiant with joy, returned to her home. Her son was surprised by the look of peace on her face. He asked, "Mom, what did you do today that made you so happy?" **"Oh my,"** she said, **"I had lunch with God and do you know he is much younger than I had expected?"**

Too often we under estimate the power of a touch . . . the radiance of a smile or the sound of a kind word. A listening ear, an honest compliment, or the smallest act of kindness. Last week my wife Audrey went to Mystic, Connecticut to have lunch with her sister-in-law. After they finished eating they decided to visit Ender's Island just a short distance away. Located on the island is a beautiful stone monastery named St. Edmund's Chapel. They wanted to see the Stations of the Cross which were done by a famous Swiss artist. While they were there they noticed an elderly woman sitting alone in a pew. It appeared that she had been crying and was very upset. As Audrey passed her seat she put her hand on the woman's shoulder and said, **"God loves you,"** and continued to walk down the aisle. On the way out the woman reached out and grasped Audrey's hand, gave it a big squeeze and with a sweet smile said, **"Thank you for your comment, I needed that so much."** Sometimes just a kind word, a sweet smile, or a friendly touch will bless both the receiver and the giver. Never under-estimate the power of your witness.

Spiritual Starvation

"How sweet are your words to my taste, sweeter than honey to my mouth?" Psalm 119: 103

We live in a country that is well fed. Doctors and health officials acknowledge that our people are fortunate to have an abundance of food in our country. Even during the off-season times we are able to get fresh fruit and vegetables from other lands, if we please. There is something exciting about having corn on the cob in mid-winter, or water melon in early spring. Living in America, with our wonderful transportation and shipping system, allows us the opportunity to have almost anything that we desire. In fact, nutritionists are concerned because Americans are over-eaters and gluttons, who fail to balance their diets and often eat the wrong kinds of food. Fast food companies are extremely aware of the problems and are working to educate the public to the facts that there are other choices of food stuffs rather than hamburgers and French fries. Personally, I have trouble getting by the Inside Dip on Ten Rod Road. I love ice cream.

That is why we may not be familiar with the symptoms of starvation. There are few cases of starvation in our land. At the onset of starvation the victims have an insatiable craving for nourishment. As time passes, however, the body weakens, the mind is dulled, and the desire for something to eat wanes. In fact, starving people actually reach a point when they don't even want food that is placed before them.

Spiritual starvation follows much the same course. If we have been feeding daily on God's Word it is natural to feel "hungry" when we miss or skip our quiet time. But, if we continue to neglect it we may lose all desire to study the scriptures. We may be starving ourselves of an important part of our lives. How much time do you spend reading the Bible and meditating on its truths? Do you miss the word when you neglect it? Thomas Guthrie wrote, "If you find yourself loving any pleasure better than your prayers, or reading any book more than the Bible, or caring more about anyone more than Christ, or you are imprudent about any indulgence more than the hope of heaven---take alarm."

If you have lost your taste for the "Bread of Life," confess your negligence and ask God to revive your appetite for His Word. Avoid spiritual starvation!

Story: Dan's daughter was complaining about how difficult her life had become. She said, "It is almost like I am starving myself to death." Dan said nothing, but took her by the hand and led her to the kitchen. He set three pans of water on the stove and brought them to a boil. He added carrots to the first pan; eggs to the second pan and coffee grounds to the third pan.

After they had cooked a short time he put the contents in separate bowls and asked his daughter to cut into the carrots and the eggs. They both could smell the aroma of the fresh coffee. "What does this mean?" she asked impatiently.

"Each food," he answered, "teaches us something about life. The carrots went in hard and came out soft. The eggs went in fragile but came out hardened. The coffee simply changed the water to something better.

If we are to survive and live we must make a choice of what we do. We must revive our appetites for His Word and avoid spiritual starvation.

A Well-Read Bible is a sign of a Well-Fed Soul.

DON'T BE A HYPOCRITE

It has been said that people often never appear as they really are. Webster defines a **hypocrite** as, "One who pretends to have a virtue, a feeling, or ability that he doesn't have." Or it might be said, it's the person who isn't himself on Sundays.

One of the most stressful things for Jesus was to have to deal with those who practiced hypocrisy. People who made the appearance of being upstanding and good yet were pretenders and deceivers to the core. Jesus called the religious leaders of His day hypocrites. (Mt. 23: 13-15). He meant they were actors who played several parts. In the ancient theaters each actor entertained using different identities and they would change that character by simply changing masks. They were putting on a performance to win the applause of the audience, but they didn't care what they were like deep inside.

Jesus instructed us not to be like hypocrites who perform their religious duties to be seen by others. (Mt. 6: 1-6). He said, "When you do a charitable deed, do not let your left hand know what your right hand is doing."

God isn't impressed by the masks we wear to get approval. Instead, He reserves His applause for those who worship Him and give themselves in love to one another.

Story: A young man by the name of Gaston went to his favorite restaurant for dinner. As he arrived, he was met by the maître d', greeted and ushered promptly to his special table. Gaston was dressed impeccably. He wore a dark blue suit, a white shirt and striped tie.

His black shoes were shined to a mirror finish. He was truly a fashion plate.

As he was seated two waiters appeared at the table. The first waiter asked for his choice of fine wines. The second waiter filled his water glass and quickly removed the extra silverware and napkins, for they knew he was dining alone. Everyone sighed and whispered. "Isn't he the good looking, successful business man who eats here so often?" Gaston quickly placed his order as the first waiter filled his wine glass. It was a perfect evening and he was the picture of charm and affluence.

Quietly and without notice someone moved a mirror to the left of where Gaston was sitting. Suddenly Gaston's image reflected a different person. There was a man with black hair slicked back wearing a black cape with a dagger in his mouth with fangs sticking out. His eyes were squinted and had turned red. He had a look of evil about him.

In all outward appearances Gaston has an outstanding, upright citizen. But in truth he was a hypocrite to the core. **He was a street angel but a home devil.**

When Jesus was talking with the scribes and Pharisees He told about Isaiah's prophesies regarding **hypocrites.**

> *"These people honor me with their lips,*
> *But their hearts are far from me.*
> *They worship me in vain: their teachings*
> *Are but rules taught by men.*
> *You have let go of the commands of God,*
> *And are holding on to the traditions of men."*
> *Mark 7:6-8*

DON'T BE A HYPOCRITE

A Grateful Heart

"They did not believe His word, but complained in their tents." Psalm 106: 24-25

Have you ever met or known someone who is a habitual complainer? Some people have turned complaining into an art form. If you were to say, "I don't have anything to complain about," they would be happy to offer some suggestions. They would count their many blessings and then complain that there weren't enough, or they needed more.

In the Old Testament of the Bible, we read about the people of Israel who had become a nation of complainers. After God had provided a safe journey for them as they departed Egypt and crossed over The Red Sea they wanted to settle down and begin to build new homes. But Moses was instructed by God to lead the people into the wilderness. The people complained about it. What would they do, where would they live, and what would they have to eat?

God provided quail and manna. But they turned up their noses at God's menu. They had gotten tired of quail and manna, a bread that was white like coriander seed and tasted like wafers made with honey. The complainers would argue, "It was good at first but you get tired of the same thing every day for forty years.

The people despised the desert, although they did move around from one oasis to another. They hated the tents in which they lived. But the tents made them a nomadic tribe, avoiding the dangers in the desert, and risks of attack by unfriendly people. They rebelled against Moses when they camped at Rephidim and there was no water for the people to drink. God gave Moses an instruction to use his staff to strike a rock, which produced water abundantly. The people still complained. To despise God's blessing is to despise God. That is why he punished the Israelites.

They were like the old gentleman who approached a young stranger in the Post Office. The older man asked the younger person to help him address a postcard. "Of course," answered the young man, "I would gladly do that." Then he offered to write a short note on the card. Finally the young man asked, "Is there anything else I can do for you?" The old man thought for a moment and said, "Yes, at the end could you add, 'Please excuse the sloppy hand writing?'"

God doesn't like complainers. He doesn't take complaining lightly. Such words despise His grace. It is far better to stop and count our blessings--to think about them and thank God for each one. Then, in addition to all He has given us, thank God for having given us a grateful heart.

> *"Now we all can thank our God,*
> *With heart and hand and voices,*
> *Who's wondrous things hath done,*
> *In whom His world rejoices."*

Gratitude is the best attitude

THE COURAGE CYCLE

I believe that we have cycles of being encouraged and discouraged. C. S. Lewis defines **courage** as, *"Not simply one of our virtues but the form of every virtue at the testing point, which means the point of highest reality."* The verb **encourage** means to give courage to or help. When you feel encouraged, you feel as though you could fly without wings. You are full of energy and take on tasks with zeal. You feel like you can accomplish the impossible.

But when you are discouraged you are listless. You feel zapped of your energy. Your boldness is drained away. Whatever power you had is gone and you feel worthless. Let's call it the **Courage Cycle.** At the peak of your courage cycle you are ready to take on the entire world. But for any number of reasons, even before the day is done you may hit the bottom of the cycle. You have become completely discouraged.

Experiencing discouragement is like feeling emotionally beat up. You feel as though your train has "jumped the track" and the rest of the world rushes on. You feel like a social failure, alone. There is the key component to discouragement; **"You feel alone."**

Everyone goes through the cycle. Everyone from your children to your friends and co-workers and your associates. They too are going to feel discouraged and when they do they will feel alone. That makes it easier to know how to encourage someone. Often all it takes is to let them know that, **"You are not alone."** and someone cares.

It can be as simple as stopping by someone's house or office and cracking a joke or telling a story. A quick e-mail can do the trick. Send a greeting card or a little note. The shortest message can be powerful medicine because it attacks discouragement at the foundation by declaring, **"You are not alone."** Greeting someone you see by their first name simply says that you care about them, they are not alone and God loves them.

The key to encouraging people--building them up, is to remind them of their strengths. Let them know that they matter and that they have an important place in the world.

What if you are discouraged? No one comes to visit you. No one helps you with encouragement. You don't get any phone calls or emails or cards. Here is a basic principle in life, **"Give and it will be given unto you."** So if you are discouraged don't wait for someone to come along and help you. Take the initiative and look around for someone else who is down and you reach out to them. Be there for them. Build them up. And a strange thing will happen. When you are there for someone else you suddenly are, **"Not alone."** Get the point? Encouraging someone else encourages you.

Interestingly, even if two discouraged people get together to have their own private "Pity Party" they end up encouraging one another because they realize that they are not alone. Perhaps that is why two people having lunch together is such an important event. Men don't know the importance of "A Girls Night Out" because it enables the ladies to share their concerns and let each other know that they are not alone. In the process don't overlook the importance of including God in your life. He will listen to your problems, share your concerns and convince you that you are not alone. Webster defines alone as, **"With no other."** God is always with us and gives us endless love. We are never along with Him.

DO ANGELS HAVE WINGS

Artists often paint pictures of angels having wings. People have written stories that describe angels having wings or earning their wings. But, the Bible doesn't say that all angels have wings. It does say that angels can fly and that, at times, they appear with wings. But angels don't need wings to fly like birds or butterflies do. God made sure that they can get to where they are needed, when they need to go.

In the book of Daniel we find this scripture: *"I (Daniel) prayed and Gabriel flew swiftly to me. He is the angel I had seen in the earlier vision." Daniel 9: 21*

Isaiah reported this in his scripture: *"I saw the Lord seated on a throne, high and exalted, and the train of his robe filled the temple. Above him were the seraphs (angels), each with six wings: With two wings they covered their faces, with two they covered their feet and with two they were flying." Isa. 6: 1-2 with* this description, we might conclude that angels do have wings.

Some questions we might ask would be: Why do Angels fly? Do Angels look like the ones we make in the snow? Do all angels have wings?

Finally, if we look up the word angel in the dictionary we will find the definition: **angel (n) is a messenger of God, pictured with wings.**

So what do you think?

CALLED ALONG SIDE

While based at the Naval Air Station, Chincoteague, Virginia I was attached to Utility Squadron Four (VU-4) as a Navy pilot. Our mission was to support the Navy in training the crews on warships to operate the anti-aircraft guns aboard their vessels.

Phase one of the training syllabus was to begin to learn and practice the use of radar tracking. We would dispatch an aircraft to the operations area, located 30 to 75 miles off shore so that the ship's crew could become proficient in tracking the target on their radar controlled guns. Phase two of the exercise was to have the airplane stream a target sleeve that was 7000 feet behind the airplane and after the Combat Information Center (CIC) Officer was satisfied that the crews were capable, he would allow them to begin firing live ammunition. Our pilots had a slogan that said, "Remember, we are pulling this target, not pushing it."

The aircraft carriers, battleships and cruisers were all very good. They would occasionally shoot the sleeve off the tow cable and we would have to stream another target in order to continue the exercise. Some of the smaller ships like supply ships, LSTs, and even some destroyers weren't as sharp or didn't have the fire power to even come close.

I remember one shoot out when the tow-aircraft, (Tractor One) was instructed to make a diving run from 4000 feet across the bow of a supply ship (AK). The pilot had to use caution to cross the bow slightly ahead of the ship and to make his approach so that the target sleeve would be about 800 to 1000 above the water. In normal level flight a 7000 foot cable will drupe 100 feet for every 1000 feet extended. In other words, with a 7000 foot cable the target is almost 700 feet below the airplane. During a dive the sleeve will not drupe as much, maybe only 300 to 400 feet. Also, when making a wide turn the sleeve tends to track to the inside radius and will actually go lower than when it is in level flight. One of the first things we learn when towing targets is to try and keep the sleeve out of the water.

On this flight the plan was to make a diving run across the bow. The plane was at 4,000 feet, the pilot started the dive and reported his action to the fire control Officer. The pilot heard the fire control officer acknowledge the report and then heard him say, "Commence firing!" Smoke rings were observed coming from the bow turret and bursts of flack began to explode in front of the airplane. The pilot took evasive action and yelled, "Cease fire, cease fire!"

Clear of the line of fire and away from the exploding shells the airplane crew began to assess the damage. None could be seen but to be on the safe side the pilot radioed to Flight Operations at Chinco that they were terminating the exercise and returning to base. He also requested that another airplane be dispatched to come up to meet them and come alongside for a closer look. It was done, no damage and the flight returned safely to base.

The action of this crew is an illustration of the ministry of Jesus and the action of the Holy Spirit. Jesus told his disciples in John 14: 16 *"I will pray to the Father, and He will give you another helper."* The word helper may also be translated "Comforter" or "Counselor." and literally means one called alongside to help.

The Holy Spirit guides us and protects us through the fire and the dangers of life, much like the observation plane that came up to look us over and to report any damage. The Spirit buffers us from all harm, whether it is emotional, physical, or spiritual. He is always there to protect, comfort, encourage and counsel. He will guide us until we are safely home

GOD'S SPIRIT LIVES INSIDE US, AND ALSO WALKS BESIDE US.

GOD LOATHES EVIL

The Bible describes God as Jehovah, a God of holiness, righteousness; just, and sovereign. These attributes tells the following about God: (1) God is capable of preventing evil, and (2) God desires to rid the universe of evil. If this it true why does He still allow evil? Why doesn't He just stop all evil? Perhaps the way to look at the question is to consider some alternative ways that God might run the world:

(1) Were d could change everyone's personality so they cannot sin. This would mean we would not have free will. We would not be able to choose right or wrong because we would be programmed to do only right. If this is were done there would be no meaningful relationship between God and His creation.

Instead, God made Adam and Eve innocent, but with ability to choose between right or wrong, to do well or do evil. He did this because He wanted them to respond to His love and trust Him. They could either obey or disobey. They chose to disobey. Because we live in a world where we can choose our actions, but not the consequences Adam and Eve's sin has an impact on us, on those around us, and those who will come after us.

(2) God could compensate for people's evil actions through divine intervention all of the time. God would stop a drunk driver from causing an automobile accident. He would stop a lazy construction worker from doing a substandard job on

a building that would cause grief or danger to the owners. He would stop a father who is addicted to drugs or alcohol from doing harm to his wife and children. God would stop a gunman from robbing a convenience store. He would stop thieves from shoplifting. God would stop wars and terrorism, and acts of inhumanity.

While the solution sounds attractive, it would lose its attractiveness the minute God intervened or infringed on something we wanted to do. We want God to prevent horribly evil actions, but we are willing to let less-evil actions slide—not realizing that they may lead to greater-evil actions. Should God stop true theft, or should He stop us from cheating on our taxes? Should He stop a speeder for exceeding the posted speed limit or just slow us down if we are attempting to get to church on time? Should God stop acts of terrorism, or should He stop the indoctrination and transforming of a person into a terrorist?

(3) Another choice would be for God to judge and remove those who commit evil acts. The problem with this is there probably wouldn't be anyone left to remove since we all sin and commit evil acts. While some people are more evil than others, where would God draw the line? Ultimately, all evil causes harm to others.

Instead of these options, God has chosen to create a world which has real choices with real consequences. In the real world our actions affect others. Adam chose to sin, and the world now lives under the curse. We are all born with a sinful nature. There will one day come a time when God will judge the sin and made all things new, but He purposely is delaying that course to allow more time for people to repent so that they will be saved. God is concerned about evil. When He created the Old Testament Laws, the goal was to discourage and punish evil. God judges nations and rulers who disregard justice and purse evil. Likewise, in the New Testament God states that the government is responsible to provide justice to protect the people fro0m sin. He promises severe consequences for those who commit evil acts, especially against the innocent.

In summary, we live in a real world where our good and evil actions have both direct and indirect consequences for us and those around us. God's desire is that for all of our sakes we would obey Him so that will be good for all. But, what happens is that we choose our own way, and we blame God for not doing anything about it. Such is the heart of the sinful man. God sent his son Jesus to change men's hearts through the power of the Holy Spirit and He does this for those who will turn from evil and let Jesus bee their guide.

God does prevent and restrain some acts of evil. This world would be **much worse** were it not for God. At the same time, God has given us the ability to choose good and evil, and when we choose evil He allows us to suffer the consequences of evil. Rather than blaming God and questioning God on why He does not prevent evil we should be proclaiming the cure for evil and its consequences---**Jesus Christ!**

SHOULD WE HONOR OR OBSERVE THE OLD TESTAMENT

If you ever wonder how **faith** fits into an increasingly corrupt and violent society you will be able to identify with the prophet Micah who wrote his book during the reigns of **Jotham, Ahaz,** and **Hezekiah,** during the years of 750 - 686 BC.

The powerful Assyrian empire was expanding westward **demanding** a surrender **and** tribute from the people living in those lands. The northern kingdom of Israel rebelled and the Assyrians destroyed the capital city of Samaria. They took many Israelites into exile. **King Hezekiah,** of the southern kingdom also rebelled against the Assyrians in 701 BC as they took his land. The Assyrians devastated Judah and carried many into captivity. When they attacked Jerusalem God delivered the city and spared the slaughter in answer to Hezekiah's prayers.

The prophet Micah wrote to the people of Judah to warn them that God's judgment was approaching because they had repeatedly rejected God and His Laws. Micah encouraged the godly few to prevail, assuring them that God's judgment would not permanently destroy Israel and that the nation would be restored.

In today's scripture Micah 6:8, we are given a clue. In order to better understand we need to review Chapter 6.

> *"Stand up, plead your case before the mountains:*
> *Let the hills hear what you have to say.*
> *Hear O mountains the Lord's accusation,*
> *Listen, you everlasting foundations of earth*

> *For the Lord has a case against His people.*
> *He is lodging a charge against Israel.*
> *My people, what have I done to you?*
> *How have I burdened you? Answer me.*
> *I brought you up out of Egypt and redeemed you*
> *From a land of slavery.*
> *I sent Moses to lead you. Also Aaron and Miriam.*
> *My people, remember what Balak, son of Beor answered.*
> *Remember your journey from Shittim to Gilgal that*
> *You may know the righteous acts of the Lord.*
> *With what shall I come before the Lord and bow down*
> *Before the exalted God?*
> *Shall I come before him with burnt offerings, with calves a*
> *Year old? Will the Lord be pleased with thousands of rams?*
> *With ten thousand rivers of oil? Shall I offer my first born?*
> *For my transgressions, the fruit of my body for the sin of*
> *my soul? He has showed you, O man what is good .And*
> *what does the Lord require of you? To act justly, and to love*
> *mercy and to walk humbly with God." Micah 6: 1-8 NIV*

And, so the question: **Should we obey or ignore the Old Testament Law?** The answer to that question is not cut and dried. The law consisted of the commands God gave Moses nearly 430 years after God established his covenant with Abraham. Apostle Paul's letter to the Church at Galatia about 48 -53 AD claims obeying the law could **not** be the basis for a relationship with God. **Faith** is the only basis for that relationship.

The Law was never intended take the place of **faith**. It was never designed to give the people of Israel a list of rules by which they could earn their salvation. Rather, the law served only to show the people how far short of God's standard they fell.

The law exposed sin so that people would be led to Christ for redemption of sin. Paul called the Law; Holy **Spiritual** and **Good**, if used properly. Otherwise, if the Law is used improperly, as a way to earn salvation, or to try to impress other people, it serves only to impose a curse.

Paul admonishes us not to ignore the Old Testament Law because it shows what God considered important. Much of it spells out the timeless principles of righteous Living. Parts of the law are still helpful for those who want to live holy lives. But Christians are not bound to fulfill the requirements of the Old Testament Law in Order to earn God's favor. Christians are to live a life of obedience to Jesus Christ and to the teachings of all Scripture, both Old and New Testament. Christians are to be strong and compliant in their **Faith.**

Paul's letter to the Galatians explains:

> *"Is the law therefore opposed to the promises of God?*
> *Absolutely not! For if a law had been given that could*
> *Impart life, then righteousness would have certainly come*
> *By the law. But scripture declares that the whole world*
> *Is a prisoner of sin, so that what was promised, being given*
> *Through the faith in Jesus Christ, might be given to whose*
> *Who believe? Before this faith came, we were held prisoners*
> *by the law. Locked up until faith should be revealed. So the*
> *law was put in charge to lead us to Christ, that we might be*
> *justified by Faith. Now that Faith has come we are no longer*
> *under the Law." Galatians 3: 21-23*

Simply said: **What does the Lord require of us?**

a. **To act justly,**
b. **Love mercy,**
c. **Have faith in Jesus Christ,**
d. **Walk humbly with God.**

Pastor Murray Hunt, preaching a short sermon to a church he was leaving said, **"Love the Lord, and do as you please."**

Holidays

A RELIGIOUS FESTIVAL USUALLY A WORK FREE DAYS

NEW YEAR'S DAY

New Year's Day is observed on January 1, the first day of the year on the modern Gregorian calendar as well as the Julian calendar used in ancient Rome. With most counties using the Gregorian calendar as their primary calendar, New Year's Day is the closest thing to being the world's only truly global public holiday. The New Year is often celebrated with fireworks at the stroke of midnight as the New Year starts January 1st.

The Romans dedicated the day to Janus, the God of gates, doors, and beginnings. After Julius Caesar reformed the calendar in 46 BC and was subsequently murdered, the Roman Senate voted to make a god of him and honor him on the first January in 42 BC to celebrate his life and his rationalized new calendar. The month originally owes its name to Janus, who had two faces, one looking forward and the other looking back. This suggests in some ways that the New Year's celebrations are founded on pagan traditions.

January 1 becomes a time for a fresh start in a new year after looking back at yesterday's reflections. The act of remembering the events of the passing year may help to alight in hope that the smoke emitted from the flames will bring new life to the world. New Year's Day is traditionally a feast, but since the turn of the century it has become an occasion to celebrate the evening before on New Year's

Eve. There are fireworks at midnight after watching the ball on the clock in Times Square drop. Joyous parties and festivities are held. It is a new year with new hope for the future.

HAVE A HAPPY AND JOYOUS NEW YEAR!

LENT

At the beginning of the 11th century it became a custom for all of the faithful to take part in a ceremony on the Wednesday, 40 days before Easter, called **Ash Wednesday**. Easter is celebrated on the first Sunday after the full moon following the vernal equinox. That date varies between the 22nd of March and the 25th of April. Easter is always on Sunday. Lent begins on Wednesday, 40 days before Easter.

Traditionally, on Ash Wednesday, the sign of the cross is made in ashes on a person's forehead as a symbol of that person's relationship with Jesus Christ. The period of **Lent** is intended to be a time when sinful activities and habits are forsaken. Perhaps you can remember some vows that you took that may have been considered acts of repentance. You may have given up eating ice cream, or having a smoke, or drinking a beer, or going to a popular Friday night movie with your friends. And you were very compliant. Forty days seemed like a long time.

Lent is a journey of reconciliation. God is not interested in our doing rituals, He is interested in our hearts. Wouldn't it be interesting if we were marked so that others could identify with our wellbeing? Since the Bible doesn't command us, or condemn us, for celebrating Lent, the Christian certainly is at liberty to prayerfully decide to observe Ash Wednesday or not. If you feel closer to the Lord by participating in, observing and celebrating the customs of Ash Wednesday and Lent, the important thing is to have a Biblical perspective. It is good to repent of sinful ways. It is also good to identify as a Christian. But we should never expect God to automatically bless us in response to our observing a ritual.

God is interested in our hearts, not in our doing rituals. Remember, God loves us because **of who God is . . . not because of anything we have or have not done.** *"Whoever believes and is baptized, will be saved, but whoever does not believe will be condemned."* **"God gives. We receive . . . . And we are blessed. The Lord is good to all, he has compassion on all hat he has made."**

ST. PATRICK'S DAY

Nestled among the religious traditions of Lent, is a holiday known as St. Patrick's Day. Saint Patrick was a Catholic priest who became revered by Christians for establishing the Catholic Church in Ireland in the fifth century AD.

Saint Patrick was born in Scotland in 387 and died in Ireland in 461 AD, at the age of 74. He is remember for his service to the church and to the citizens of the land. His anniversary is celebrated each year on March 17. Although the details of his life are unclear, most agree that he played a significant role in establishing Christianity in Ireland.

Lent is a period of fasting and a time for repentance traditionally observed by Catholics and some Protestant denominations, in preparation for Easter. The Lenten period was instituted in the **4th century** and has become a time of religious worship occurring 40 days before Easter. During this time people eat sparingly and give-up particular foods or habits. Ash Wednesday and Lent began as a way to remind people to repent of their sins in a manner similar to the way people in the Old Testament times repented. The use of the sackcloth, ashes, and fasting was the tradition.

Saint Patrick, born in Scotland, of religious Roman Catholic parents, was captured as a young boy of 16 years and sold into slavery in Ireland. He tended sheep for his very cruel master in the valley of Braid and on the slopes of Slemish. During his captivity, while tending the flocks, he prayed many times a day: **"The love of God."** As his prayer life grew he told of what happened: His fear (the Lord's faith) increased in him more and more, the faith grew, the spirit was roused, so that in a single day he would say as many as a 100 or more prayers, and at night nearly the same number. He claimed that he felt no hurt from it, even with snow and ice or rain there was no slothfulness, because the spirit was fervent within him.

The beautiful prayer of St. Patrick is popularly known as **"St. Patrick's Breast-Plate."** and is translated from the old Irish text.

St. Patrick's Breast- Plate
I bind to myself today
God's Power to guide me.
God's Might to uphold me,
God's Wisdom to teach me,
God's Eye to watch over me,
God's Ear to hear me,
God's Word to give me speech,
God's Hand to guide me,
God's Way to lie before me,
God's Shield to shelter me,
God's Host to secure me
Against the snare of demons.
Against the seductions of vice,
Against the lusts of nature,
Against everyone who meditates
Injury to me, whether far or near,
Whether few or many
Amen

About 432, St. Patrick returned to Ireland as a missionary and succeeded in converting many of the pagan tribes in the country to Christianity. Later in his life he wrote a brief text telling of his life and ministry. It is known as, *"The Confession of St. Patrick."*

St. Patrick's Day is a feast day in March and is celebrated as a day of **Irish Pride.** A popular folk tale says that St. Patrick chased all of the snakes from Ireland. But, there is no historical basis for this story. Another folk tale is that he used shamrocks to teach about the holy Trinity. Another myth. In Gaelic the saint's name is *Padraig.*

Whether Catholic or not, I believe that we can all benefit by knowing of St. Patrick and living the examples that he set as we say his prayer. Bless us all dear Lord.

THE LENTEN LESSON

Many Christians wonder about the traditions and events leading up to **Easter.** We learn of the events that tell **of the crucifixion of Jesus Christ, but** if we go to the scriptures and try to find details we may not find a great deal of information on the various days of Lent. Of course we can find accounts of the **Last Supper** in the four Gospels, **Matthew, Mark, Luke and John.** But we would find little about Shrove **Tuesday, Ash Wednesday, and Laetare Sunday, Maundy Thursday, and Good Friday. If** we were to look up the word Easter in our King James Bible or in any of the modern translations we might be surprised to find that the word cannot be found.

Easter was originally the festival of *Eostre,* who was an Anglo-Saxon goddess. In Acts 12:4 we can find a mistranslation for the word **Passover,** which we know as a Jewish Feast. Easter is now observed by many Christian churches in commemoration of our Savior's death, burial and resurrection. Which occurred just after the Passover and about the same time of the year as the heathen festival of *Eostre.*

In 325 AD the Council of Nicaea ruled that **Easter** should be celebrated on the first Sunday after the full moon following the vernal equinox. The date of Easter varies between the 22nd of March and the 25th of April. This year Easter is on A 20th. Therefore, Lent is March 5th, which is forty days before Easter, (Not counting Sundays, or the Lord's Day.)

The Bible contains numerous accounts of people using "dust and ashes" as a symbol of repentance and mourning. One example is Daniel, God's prophet who said:

**"Then I turned to the Lord and prayed and ask Him
For help. I did not eat any food. To show my sadness
I put on a rough cloth and sat in ashes. I prayed to the**

At the beginning of the 11ᵗʰ century it became a custom in the church for all of the faithful to take part in **a** ceremony on the Wednesday, known as Ash Wednesday. In the Christian calendar, we find a day known as **Shrove Tuesday.** This is the day before **Ash Wednesday.** It is also known as Pancake **Day.** The Name Shrove comes from the English verb **"shrive" which** means, to absolve the People of their sins. It is another way of using up the milk and eggs and flour prior to the beginning of **Lent.** Ingredients that are not consumed during the Lenten period are considered to be unrighteous.

Lent begins with Ash Wednesday. There are 40 days between Lent and **Easter.** Traditionally, during this time Christians observe the period by fasting, avoiding festivities, and performing acts of penance. Meat, fish eggs and milk products were strictly forbidden and only one meal a day was eaten. Making the sign of the cross in ashes on a person's forehead was a symbol of that person's identification with Jesus Christ.

Ash Wednesday is not a *holy day of obligation for* many congregations, but many people would not think of letting Ash Wednesday go by without a trip to church to be marked with ashes on their forehead. Since the Bible doesn't command or condemn the procedure, a Christian is at liberty to prayerfully decide to observe Ash Wednesday, or not. If you feel led to the Lord to observe Ash Wednesday and Lent, the important thing is to have a Biblical perspective. It is good to repent of sinful ways. It is also good to identify yourself as a Christian. But, we should never believe that

God will automatically bless us in response to the observing of a ritual.

God is interested in our hearts, not in our doing rituals. Remember, God loves us because of who God is, not because of anything we have or have not done.

> Three things in life that when they are gone never return. . . **Time, Words, and opportunity.**

> Three things in life that are never certain. . . **Fortune, Success, and Dreams.**

> Three things that make a person significant. . . . **Commitment, Sincerity and Hard work.**

Laetare Sunday is the fourth Sunday in Lent, marking the half-way point of Lent.

Palm Sunday. The Sunday before Easter is the beginning of Holy Week and we know that is the day that Jesus made his triumphal entry into Jerusalem, passing through the **Golden Gate.** As it was prophesied, he entered riding on a young colt and the people greeted him with palm branches, so is known as **Palm Sunday.**

The people expected the messiah to become their new King and free them from the Roman bondage. While Jesus was in Jerusalem he cleansed the temple, and cursed the fig tree. He was anointed and learned of the sinister plot that would send him to the cross.

Maundy Thursday. The fifth day of holy week when Jesus met with his disciples in the **Upper Room** for the Passover dinner. At this time Jesus established the **Lord's Supper** as recorded in Matthew 26: 17-29. The day is known as **Maundy Thursday.** Maundy Thursday marks the time that Jesus was betrayed by Judas and was arrested by the government soldiers. Christians celebrate Jesus by taking communion on this day. **Mark 14: 21-25.**

Good Friday is a holy day shared by Christians on the Friday before Easter. It preserves the memory of the pain and suffering of the crucifixion of Jesus. He was treated like a criminal, purged and beaten, mocked and rejected by the people. He was hung on the cross, and he died for our sins. It was the day Jesus Christ gave his life for remission of sin, and gave us the promise of eternal life.

> *"Whoever believes and is baptized will be saved, but whoever does not believe will be condemned." Mark 16:16*

Easter is the day that we celebrate the resurrection. As prophesied, Jesus arouse from the grave and proved that he is the Son of God. He defeated death. He fulfilled prophesy and he gave us the promise of everlasting life.

**Ask God to continue to bless us in our
Christian walk through Life.**

SHROVE TUESDAY

Shrove Tuesday is known by several other names; **Pancake Day, Pancake Tuesday, Mardi Gras,** and **Fat Tuesday.** It is the day before Ash Wednesday, the first day of Lent. Shrove Tuesday is observed mainly in English speaking counties but is also observed in the Philippines and Germany. Shrove Tuesday is linked to **Easter,** so the date changes each year. Shrove Tuesday is always the day prior to Ash Wednesday which begins a period of fasting and a time of repentance.

The word shrove is past tense of the English verb shrive, which means to obtain absolution for one's sins through confession and doing penance. Shrove Tuesday gets its name from the shriving that English Christians were expected to do in preparation for Lent. They expected to receive absolution before Lent began. Shrove Tuesday is the last day of "Shrovetide" and is somewhat analogous to a *Carnival* tradition that developed in countries of Latin America and Europe. For 'example Mardi Gras. The term **"Shrove Tuesday"** is seldom used in the UA outside of liturgical traditions. It may be better known as Pancake Day, Mardi gras, or Fat Tuesday.

In most societies, the day is better known for the custom of eating pancakes before the start of Lent. Pancakes are chosen to be eaten because they are made from ingredients consisting of sugar, fat, milk, flour and eggs. Consumption of these rich foodstuffs was inconsistent with the traditionally restricted diets during the ritual fasting associated with Lent. The liturgical fasting dictated eating plainer foods and refraining from eating foods that would give pleasure. In many cultures this means no meat, no dairy products and no eggs. The fasting season lasted 40 days, from Ash Wednesday till Easter.

Many churches take advantage of Pancake Day and host fund-raising suppers consisting of pancakes, ham and sausages. Usually these dinners are well attended and are very successful but the purpose of making money exceeds the intent of Christians preparing to fast during Lent.

ASH WEDNESDAY

Ash Wednesday is the day that **Lent begins**. **Ash Wednesday** is not a holy *day of obligation, but* many people would not think of letting Ash Wednesday go by without a trip to church to be marked with an ashen cross on their foreheads. Even people who seldom go to church at other times of the year may make a concerted effort to come for the ashes.

The official name of Ash Wednesday is the **"The Day of Ashes"**. The reason the day became known as Ash Wednesday is that it is forty days before **Good Friday,** and will always be on a Wednesday. The Bible does not mention either Lent or Ash Wednesday, but the Bible does tell of the acts of repentance and supplication that were made by God fearing people.

The period of Lent is intended to be a time when sinful activities and habits are forsaken. **Ash Wednesday** is the "commencement" of this period of repentance. Perhaps you can remember some acts of repentance that you did. You may have given up eating ice cream or having a smoke, or drinking a beer, giving up going to the popular Friday Night movie, or eating that favorite dessert. And you were very compliant. Forty days is a long time.

The Bible contains numerous accounts of people using "dust and ashes" as a symbol of repentance and/or mourning. One example is Daniel, God's prophet who said:

> *"Then I turned to the Lord God and*
> *prayed and asked Him*
> *For help. I did not eat any food. To*
> *show my sadness I put on*

182

Rough cloth and sat in ashes. I prayed
to the Lord my God and
Told him about all of my sins." Daniel 9:3

At the beginning of the 11th century it became a custom for all of the faithful to take part in a ceremony on the Wednesday before Lent that included the imposition of ashes. The tradition is that the sign of the cross is made in ashes on a person's forehead as a symbol of that person's identification with Jesus Christ. Ash Wednesday, along with Lent is observed by most Roman Catholics, most Orthodox denominations and a number of Protestant denominations. Since the Bible does not command or condemn the procedure, a Christian is at liberty to prayerfully decide whether to observe **Ash Wednesday** or not. If you feel led by the Lord to observe Ash Wednesday and/or Lent the important thing is to have a Biblical perspective. It is good to repent of sinful activities. It is good to clearly identify yourself as a Christian. But we should not believe that God will automatically bless us in response to the observing of a ritual. **God is interested in our hearts, not in our doing rituals.**

Remember that God loves us because of **who God is**, not because of **anything we did or did not do.**

Three things in Life that, once they are gone never come back:

1. Time
2. Words
3. Opportunity.

Three things in life that are never certain:

1. Fortune
2. Success
3. Dreams

Three things that make a person's life significant:

1. Commitment
2. Sincerity
3. Hard work

Three things that are truly constant:
FATHER, - SON – HOLY SPIRIT.

"I ask the Lord to bless you, as I prayed for you today,
To guide you and protect you, as you go along your way.
God's love is always with you,
God's promises are true,
And when you give God all your cares,
You know that God will see you through."

LAETARE SUNDAY

Laetare Sunday is a name often used to denote the fourth Sunday of the season of Lent in the Christian liturgical calendar. This Sunday is also known as **Mothering Sunday, Refreshment Sunday, Mid-Lent Sunday and Rose Sunday.**

Rose Sunday was named Rose Sunday because the golden rose sent by the Pope to Catholic sovereigns used to be blessed at that the time, or because the clergy could use rose-colored vestments instead of the usual violet ones. The term Laetare Sunday is used predominantly, though not exclusively, by Roman Catholics and some Anglicans. Some American Baptist Churches who recognize Lent will honor Laetare Sunday with rose colored vestments. The word Laetare translated from the Latin *Laetare,* singular imperative of *Laetare, meaning* "To rejoice.

This Sunday was also once known as the **"Sunday of the Five Loaves."** from the traditional Gospel of Mathew 14: 13-21, the story of the miracle of the loaves and fishes and the feeding of 5000. This scripture was read in the Lutheran, Anglican, Roman Catholic and Western-Rite Orthodox churches.

In many of these churches there may be flowers on the high altar, the organ may be played as a solo instrument and the priests are given the option to wear rose-colored vestments.

The day is a day of relaxation from normal Lenten rigors. It is a day of hope with Easter coming in another four weeks. Come Monday the Lenten rituals begin again

Events of Easter

Ash Wednesday: Lent begins with the ceremony of marking the forehead with ashes.

Laetare Sunday: The mid-point of Lent. Four weeks until Easter.

Palm Sunday: Marks the triumphal entry of Jesus into Jerusalem Through the Golden Gate riding a donkey colt.

Maundy Thursday: Passover dinner and Jesus establishes the Lord's Supper.

Good Friday: Jesus is betrayed by Judas, followed by a trial, the crucifixion, death and, burial in the tomb.

Resurrection Day   Mary Magdalene and the other Mary go to the tomb to prepare the body and discover the stone was rolled away and Jesus had risen.

GOOD FRIDAY

The phrase "Good Friday" does not appear in the Bible and neither does the word "Friday." The only day of the week given a name in the scriptures is the seventh day, The Sabbath. Other days of the week are designated as the first, second third and so on.

The term **Good Friday** is called by various names in different countries; Holy Friday, Black Friday, Great Friday, Long Friday and Silent Friday. According to Catholic dogma, which has been carried over into Protestant Churches, Jesus was killed on Friday and resurrected on Sunday morning.

Good Friday is a day of fasting created by the Roman Catholic Church in the 4th century A.D. (long after Jesus had died). The day is dedicated to commemorating the crucifixion and death of Jesus. Fasting consisted of eating only one meal a day but could be supplemented by small collations.

We experience the observances of Holy Week as we move from the joyous celebrations of Palm Sunday to the resurrection of our Lord. We are called to focus on the triumphal entry of Jesus through the Golden Gate into the city, followed by the suffering the humiliation, and death that is part of Holy Week.

It is important for us to place the propriety of the Resurrection and the promise of newness and everlasting life, against the background of death and endings. It is only in walking through the shadows and the darkness of Holy Week, recalling the sacrifices of Jesus on that fateful day we call Good Friday, that we can realize the horror and magnitude of sin and its consequences and how they were satisfied by the dying of Jesus on the cross. Thus we truly understand the light and the hope of Sunday morning, Resurrection Day.

There were a variety of events that clustered on the last day before Jesus was arrested. **Maundy Thursday.** The term Maundy comes from the Latin word *man datum (from which we get our English word mandate.)* It was here that Jesus washed the disciples' feet to illustrate humility and servant hood. Then the last meal, which the disciples thought was the Passover meal was eaten. It was here that Jesus established the **Lord's Supper.** But he was betrayed by Judas, for thirty Pieces of silver. The disciples were puzzled and were asking if it was one of them. Even as Jesus and his disciples came together to share the meal they already stood in the shadow of the cross. Jesus made a new covenant, as written in the scriptures. John 13:34 **Jesus said: "A new commandment I give to you. . . 'Love one another, as I have loved you. So you must love one another. By this all men will know that you are my disciples, if you have love for one another.'" John 13:34**

The scriptures tell us that after they had eaten they sang some hymns and then went out to the Garden of Gethsemane to pray. It was there that the soldiers came and arrested Jesus. He was taken to the house of the High Priest, Caiaphas, and persecuted. The High Priest didn't want Jesus' blood on his hands so he turned him over to Pontius Pilate, the governor who asked the people what they desired, and they shouted, **Crucify Him. Crucify Him, Crucify Him.**

Beaten and scourged, mocked and insulted, tortured and made to carry his cross to Calvary Hill, Jesus was treated as a lowly criminal. He was nailed to the cross and placed between two other victims of the government. Good Friday services are often a series of Scripture readings which include the following as recorded in the Gospel traditions: The last words of Jesus on the cross:

> **"Father, forgiven them for they know**
> **not what they do." Luke 23:34**
> **"I tell you the truth this day you will be**
> **with me in paradise." Luke 23: 43**

"Dear woman, here is your son." John 19:26-27
"My God, my God why have you
forsaken me?" Matthew 27:46
"I thirst" John 19:28
"It is finished!" John 19:30
"Father into your hands I commit
my spirit." Luke 23:46 NIV

At 3 PM Jesus died. Good Friday is not a day of celebration but of mourning, both for the death of Jesus and the sins of the world that his death represents. Yet, although Friday is a solemn time it is not without its own joy. For while it is important to place the resurrection against the darkness of Good Friday, likewise the somberness of Good Friday should always be seen with the hope and joy of Resurrection Sunday.

Halleluiah He Lives, Our Savior Lives.

EASTER SUNDAY

Easter was originally the festival of **Esotery**, an Anglo-Saxon goddess, and in Acts 12:4 is a mistranslation for Passover the Jewish feast. The word Easter is not found in the King James edition of the Bible nor in many translations of the modern Bible used today. Easter is observed by many Christians in commemoration of our Savior's resurrection, which occurred just after the Passover and about the same time of the year as the festival of Esotery.

Many Christians wonder about the traditions and customs of worship events leading up to Easter We all have learned about how Jesus was crucified in Jerusalem after He was condemned by Pontius Pilate. How the people seemed to turn against him and how he died on a wooden cross at Calvary, a hill called Golgotha. Golgotha means "The place of the skull."

The crucifixion of Jesus full-fills prophecy. God and Jesus knew exactly what had to be done and it was done. However, a number of things happened leading up to this time. Through the ages the church has established a number of "holy days", and events that lead to that fateful day in Jerusalem.

In the 11th century there was custom started by the church for all of the faithful to take part in a ceremony that we know as Ash Wednesday. This a time 40 days before Easter and is known as the beginning of Lent. During this time Christians observed the period by fasting, avoiding festivities, and performing acts of penance. Meat, fish, eggs, and milk products were strictly forbidden and only one meal a day was eaten. The making of a sign of the cross on a person's forehead was a symbol that the person identified with Jesus Christ.

Ash Wednesday Is not a high holy day or a day of obligation, but many Christian Church goers would not think of letting Ash Wednesday go by without a trip to church to be marked with the ashes. Since the Bible doesn't command or condemn the procedure a believer is at liberty to prayerfully decide to observe this Day if they wish. The important thing is to have a Biblical perspective. It is always good to repent of sinful ways, and it is good to identify yourself as a Christian. However, we should never believe that God will automatically bless us in response to observing a ritual. *God is interested in our hearts, not in our rituals. Remember, God loves us because of who God is. . . .Not because of anything we have or have not done.*

Three things in life that once they are gone never come back. . . .

Time, words, and opportunity.
* Three things in life are never certain. . . . . .
Fortune, Success, and dreams.
* Three things that make a person significant . . . . .
Commitments, Sincerity, and hard work.

The Sunday before Easter is Palm Sunday. It marks the beginning of **Holy Week.** We know Palm Sunday was the day that Jesus made a triumphal entry into Jerusalem through the Golden Gate. The account was beautifully described by Matthew in Chapter 20: 17-19.

> *"While Jesus was going up to Jerusalem, he took the twelve disciples aside by themselves, and said to them on the way, 'See we are going up to Jerusalem and the Son of Man will be handed over to the chief priests and scribes and they will condemn him to death; they will hand him over to the Gentiles to be mocked and flogged and crucified; and on the third day he will be raised."* Matthew 20: 17-19 NIV

191

And, as prophesied, he entered the city riding on a young colt. The people greeted Him with palm branches for they expected a new king, a messiah who would free them from the Roman bondage. While Jesus was in the city he went to the temple and drove out the money lenders and merchants. He cursed the fig tree. He was anointed and he learned more of the sinister plot to send him to the cross. On Thursday he instructed his disciples to prepare the Passover Meal. They met them in a place known as the Upper Room. It was here that Jesus instituted the **Lord's Supper.**

Matthew 26:26 tells us:

"While they were eating Jesus took a loaf of bread, and after blessing it he broke it, gave it to his disciples and said, 'Take, eat, this is my body.' Then he took the cup and after giving thanks he gave it to them, saying, 'Drink from it all of you; for this is my blood of the covenant, which is poured out for many for the forgiveness of sins. I tell you I will never again drink of this fruit of the vine until that day when I drink it new with you in my Father's kingdom."

When they had sung a hymn they went out to the Mount of Olives. Then the **betrayal.** Judas, one of Jesus' disciples, had sold out for 30 pieces of silver. The soldiers came and with a kiss from Judas the Son of Man was arrested and taken into custody. Jesus was taken before the high court and Caiaphas, the high priest began the inquiry. The charge was blasphemy, giving false witness. The court decided to find him guilty and condemned him to death.

The next morning Jesus was taken to the Governor, Pontius Pilate. Pilate was a politician. He wanted peace in the territory at any price. After a number of questions, that Jesus refused to answer, Pilate washed his hands of the matter and turned Jesus over to the people to crucify him.

Jesus was beaten and flogged and made to carry his cross up the hill to Calvary. And alongside two other criminals he was hung on the cross. From noon until three in the afternoon darkness came over the land. And Jesus was heard to say "Eli, Eli le-ma sa- bach-tha-ni. "My God, My God, why have you forsaken me? Then the curtains of the temple were torn in two, the earth shook and rocks were spit as Jesus took his final breath.

Because the Sabbath law required the body be taken down from the cross and be buried before sunset a rich man by the name of Arimathea volunteered his tomb for internment.

The government appointed guards to standby the tomb to secure its entrance. On Sunday, the first day of the week, Mary Magdalene and the other Mary went to the tomb but before they arrived an earthquake occurred and the stone was rolled away. When they looked into the tomb expecting to see Jesus' body they found the tomb was empty. Jesus had risen as he said he would. He Lives!

MEMORIAL DAY

Memorial Day was originally called **Decoration Day** when it first began. It is a day of remembrance for those who have died in our nation's service. There are many stories as to its actual beginnings, with more than two dozen towns and cities throughout the USA claiming to be the birth place of Memorial **Day.**

There is evidence that there was an organized group of women from the South that were decorating graves even before the end of the Civil War. A hymn written in **1867 entitled**. *"Kneel Where Our Loves Are Sleeping,"* by Neola L Sweet, credits the ladies of the South for decorating the graves of the fallen Confederate dead.

Memorial Day was officially proclaimed on May **5, 1868** by General John Logan, National Commander of the Grand Army of the Republic. General Logan's *Order No. 11* was first observed on May 30, 1868 by placing flowers on the graves of both Union and Confederate soldiers at Arlington National Cemetery.

The first State to officially recognize the holiday was New York, in 1873. By 1890 it was recognized by all of the northern states. The southern states refused to acknowledge the day and continued to honor their dead on separate days until after World War I. When the holiday changed from honoring those who died fighting in the Civil War to honoring every **American** who died fighting in all wars.

Memorial Day is now celebrated, by almost every State, on the last Monday in May. A bill was enacted by Congress in **1971,** which made it a three day weekend and a Federal Holiday throughout the entire country.

In 1915, inspired by a poem *"In Flanders Fields",* by **John McCrae,** a young woman by the name of **Molina Michael,** added this prophetic verse:

"We cherish too. The poppy red.
That grows on fields where valor led,
It seems to signal to the skies
That blood of heroes never dies."

Molina Michael conceived an idea to wear red poppies on **Memorial Day,** in honor of those who died serving the nation during war. She was the first to wear a red poppy and sold poppies to her friends and co-workers. With the money that was raised going to benefit servicemen and their families who were in need.

Madam Guerin from France, visiting the United States, learned of this new custom and when she returned to France she began making artificial red poppies to raise money for war orphans and widows in her country. The tradition spread to other countries in Europe and by 1921 it had become a tradition. Madam Guerin approached the VFW with her plan and they became the first veteran's group to sell poppies nationally. The tradition continues to this day.

Traditional observances of **Memorial Day** has seemed to diminish over the years. Many Americans have forgotten the meaning of Memorial Day. At many cemeteries the graves of the fallen are increasingly ignored and neglected. Most people no longer remember the proper flag etiquette for the day. People look to Memorial Day as a three day weekend holiday. But there are still towns and cities that continue to hold Memorial Day parades and ceremonies. Our own Rhode Island Veterans Cemetery has a spectacular display of flags on Memorial Day. We should be proud of our heritage and keep it alive.

In 1951 the **Boy Scouts of America** began placing flags on the grave sites of the servicemen and women in our national cemeteries. The scouts from Troop 2 East Greenwich, place flags on each of the graves in the Rhode Island Veterans Cemetery. A great tribute to our veterans and an act of patriotism by the scouts.

What we need to do is to re-establish the solemn, sacred **spirit of Memorial Day.** Make it our traditional day of observance of our service men and women. The day that we honor our fallen heroes. In keeping with our **Memorial Day** celebration I would like to share with you the poem written by John McRae, entitled, **"In Flanders Fields".** The poem was written by a young Army surgeon who had witnessed the battle and carnage that took place in France at Flanders Field in World War I. It inspired him to write this poem that pays tribute to those who died. The verse admonishes us to never forget to continue to carry the torch and to keep the faith that those who died were not in vain.

In Flanders Fields

In Flanders Fields the poppies grow.
Between the crosses, row by row,
That mark the place; and in the sky,
The larks still bravely, singing fly.

Scarce heard amid the guns below.
We are the dead. Short days ago.
We lived, fell down, saw sunset glow.
Loved and were loved, and now we lie
In Flanders Fields.
Take up our quarrel with the foe:
To you from falling hands we throw,
The torch: Be yours to hold on high,
If ye break faith with us who die,
We shall not sleep while poppies grow.
In Flanders Fields. John McRae

Traditional observances of Memorial **Day** has seemed to diminish over the years. Many Americans have forgotten the meaning of Memorial Day. At many cemeteries the graves of the fallen are increasingly ignored and neglected. Most people no longer remember the proper flag etiquette for the day. People look to Memorial Day as a three day weekend holiday. But there are still people in towns and cities who continue to hold Memorial Day parades and ceremonies. Our own Rhode Island Veterans Cemetery has a spectacular display of flags on Memorial Day. We should be proud of our heritage and keep it alive.

In 1951 the **Boy Scouts of America** began placing flags on the grave sites of servicemen and women in our national cemeteries. The scouts from Troop 2, East Greenwich, place flags on each of the graves in the Rhode Island Veterans Cemetery. A great tribute to our veterans and an act of patriotism by the Boy Scouts of America.

What must we do to re-establish the solemn, sacred spirit of **Memorial Day?** Make it our traditional day of observance of our service men and women. The day that we honor our fallen heroes. In keeping with our Memorial **Day** celebration I would recommend reading the poem written by John McRae, entitled, "**In Flanders Fields**". The poem was written by a young Army surgeon who had witnessed the battle and carnage that took place in France at Flanders Field in World War I. It inspired him to write a poem that pays tribute to those who died. The verse admonishes us to never forget to continue to carry the torch and to keep the faith that those who died were not in vain.

We need to acknowledge and praise God for having allowed us the freedom that we enjoy, and give honor and thanks to our brothers and sisters who gave their lives in our behalf.

> *"May the Lord direct your hearts into God's love and Christ's Perseverance?*

2 Thessalonians

INDPENDENCE DAY

Pledge Of Allegiance

Independence Day, commonly known as the **Fourth of July,** is a federal holiday in the United States commemorating that day in 1776 when the people of this land declared their independence from the King of Great Britain. Independence Day is commonly associated with fireworks, parades, barbecues, carnivals, fairs, picnics, concerts, baseball games, reunions and patriotic speeches.

During the American Revolution the legal separation of the Thirteen Colonies from Great Britain actually occurred on **July 2, 1776**, when the Continental Congress voted to approve a resolution that had been proposed earlier in June by Richard Henry Lee of Virginia.

After voting for **independence** the Congress turned its attention to the **Declaration of Independence a** document that explains their decision, which had been prepared by a committee of five, with Thomas Jefferson as its principal author. Congress debated and revised the Declaration, several times, finally approving it on the **Fourth of July.**

There are many customs and traditions that can be recalled about the 4th of July, including some of the following:

- The observance that began in 1777 when thirteen gunshots were fired in salute in the morning and again in the evening at dusk on the 4th began in Bristol, Rhode Island.
- Philadelphia celebrated the first 4th of July in a manner with which we can identify. They had a dinner for the Continental

Congress, complete with toasts 13-gun salutes, speeches, prayers, and music, parades, troops passing in review, and of course, lots of fireworks.

In 1778, General George Washington marked the day by declaring a double ration of rum for his soldiers and an artillery salute firing out over the Atlantic Ocean.

- In 1779, July 4th fell on a Sunday. The holiday was celebrated on Monday, July 5th. Now we celebrate Independence Day on the fourth of July regardless of the day of the week.

- In 1785 the Bristol, Rhode Island 4th of July parade began and it is the oldest continuous Independence Day celebration in the United States.

And we can go on and on recalling the notable events and occasions that we remember about the 4th of July. But, there is one thing that we must acknowledge and that is without God's blessing our nation would never be what it is today.

We may think that the **Pledge of Allegiance** does not fit with the theme of the Fourth of July. If so, you need to know this true story that will help you understand that it does.

Senator John McCain, Senator from Arizona and former candidate for the Presidency of the United States tells of his experience as a Navy pilot being shot down over North Vietnam in 1968:

"As you may know, I spent five and one half years as a prisoner of war during the Vietnam War. In the early years of our imprisonment the North Vietnamese Army kept us in solitary confinement, but never more than two or three men to a cell.

In 1971 the NVA moved us from these conditions of isolation to larger rooms with as many as 30 to 40 men to a room. This was, as you can imagine, a wonderful change and was a direct result of the efforts of millions of Americans helping from home.

One of the men who moved into my room was a young man named Mike Christian. Mike came from a small town near Selma, Alabama.

Mike didn't wear a pair of shoes until he was 13 years old. At age 17 he enlisted in the U.S. Navy. He advanced in his rank and earned a commission by going to Officer Cadet School. Then he became a Navy Flight Officer. He was shot down and captured in 1967.

Mike had a keen and deep appreciation for the opportunities this country and our military has for people who want to work and want to succeed. As part of the change in treatment, the Vietnamese allowed some prisoners to receive packages from home. In many of these packages were handkerchiefs, scarves and other items of clothing.

Mike got himself a bamboo needle and over a period of several months he created an American flag and sewed it to the inside of his shirt. Every afternoon, before we had a bowl of soup, we would hang Mike's shirt on the wall of the cell and say the Pledge of Allegiance.

I know the Pledge of Allegiance may not seem the most important part of our day now, but I can assure you that in that stark cell block it was indeed the most important and meaningful event.

One day the Vietnamese searched our cell, as they did periodically and discovered Mike's shirt with the flag sewn inside, and removed it. That evening they returned, opened the door of the cell and for the benefit of us beat Mike Christian severely for the next couple of hours. Then, they opened the door of the cell and threw him in. We cleaned him up as well as we could.

The cell in which we lived had a concert slab in the middle on which we slept. Four naked light bulbs hung in each corner of the room. As I said, we tried to clean Mike up as well as we could. After the excitement died down, I looked in the corner of the room, and sitting there beneath that dim light bulb with a piece of red cloth, another shirt and his bamboo needle was my friend, Mike Christian. He was sitting there with his eyes almost shut from the beating he had received, making another American flag. He was not making the flag because it made Mike Christian feel better. He was making that flag because he knew how important it was to be able to **Pledge Allegiance** to the flag of our country.

So as we say the **Pledge of Allegiance** we must never forget the sacrifice and courage that thousands of Americans have made to build our nation and promote freedom around the world. We must always remember our duty, our honor and our belief in our country.

"I pledge allegiance to the flag of the United States of America, and to the republic for which it stands, one nation under God, indivisible, with liberty and justice for all."

HANUKKAH

Hanukkah is a Hebrew verb meaning "to dedicate", and is often Romanized as *Chanukah, Chanukahs* or *Chanukah, It* is known as the **Festival of Lights.** The festival is an eight-day Jewish holiday commemorating the re-dedication of the second Holy Temple in Jerusalem.

Judea was part of the Ptolemaic Kingdom until 200 BC, when the King of Syria defeated King Ptolemy V of Egypt, to take over Judea and make it part of the Seleucid Empire of Syria. King Antiochus III wanted to conciliate his new Jewish subjects so he guaranteed their right to "live according to their ancestral customs" and to continue to practice their religion in the Temple of Jerusalem.

In 175 BC, the King's son, Antiochus IV invaded Judea at the request of a group of Jews named Tobias who wanted Antiochus IV to recapture Jerusalem. He complied marched on Jerusalem with a great army and took the city by force, slaying multitudes that favored the former Egyptian rulers. Antiochus IV ordered his soldiers to plunder, burn and destroy without mercy. He also spoiled the Temple, putting a stop to the practice of daily offerings and sacrifice of expiation. This lasted for three years and six months.

When the Temple in Jerusalem was looted and desecrated Judaism was outlawed in 167 BC. Antiochus even ordered an altar to Zeus erected in the Temple. He banned circumcision and provoked a large scale revolt.

The temple was liberated and rededicated. The festival **Hanukkah** was instituted **to** celebrate the event. Judah ordered the Temple to be cleansed, a new altar to be built and new holy vessels to be made. Olive oil was needed to fuel the menorah candles which were required to burn night and day. There was only enough olive oil to burn for one day, yet it burned for eight days, the time needed to prepare a fresh supply of oil for the menorah. As a result an eight day festival was declared by the Jewish sages to commemorate this miracle.

Hanukkah is celebrated by a series of rituals that are performed every day throughout the eight day period. Some are family-based and others are communal. There is no obligation to refrain from activities that are forbidden on the "Sabbath-like" holidays.

Fried foods are traditionally eaten on Hanukkah in commemoration of the oil that miraculously burned for eight days when the Maccabees purified and rededicated the Holy Temple in Jerusalem. Fried potato pancakes (called Latkes in Yiddish, and Levivot in Hebrew) are hands down, mouth-open favorites of the holiday.

Hanukkah begins on November 27 this year and will last until December 3. This year, 2013, Hanukkah falls on Thanksgiving Day, November 28. The last time this has occurred was 1888. It will not happen again for 7000 years, according to the Jewish calendar.

Thanksgiving and Hanukkah both have religious connotations, and both have festive connections. Hanukkah is a time for celebrating the re-dedication of the temple in Jerusalem in 175 BC. It is a time for thanking God who mysteriously supplied the olive oil to light the menorah for eight days and provide cooking oil for the people. The Jew fled religious beliefs and persecution as they rebelled against the process of worshipping false Gods and idols.

The first Thanksgiving was a celebration by the Pilgrims at Plymouth Plantation for a successful and plentiful year of 1621. They thanked God for His blessing and watch care as they came to the New World to avoid the dictates of the Church of England.

Likewise, we continue the tradition of Thanksgiving to offer thanks to God for all that we receive through His bounty.

THANKSGIVNG

Harvest Festival

Thanksgiving Day is a harvest festival. It is a time to give thanks for that which we have Canada. While it has a **religious** origin, Thanksgiving is principally identified as a **secular holiday.** That is to do with the things of the world, not spiritual or under church control.

It seems like the month of November is a bridge between two of the biggest commercial events of the year--**Halloween** and **Christmas**, with **Thanksgiving** stuck right in the middle. For many, Thanksgiving is a melody of **over eating;** gluttonous meals; turkey and dressing, cranberry sauce, mash-potatoes and gravy, including corn pudding, sweet potatoes, green beans, squash, followed by pumpkin pie or pecan pie with whipped cream. Hum, makes you hungry to think about it. Did you know that more than 300 million turkeys are raised in the United States each year with an estimated 40 million consumed on Thanksgiving Day? Then it seems like the day in concluded with long naps, or watching football games on TV.

In **1621**, after a hard and devastating first year in the New World, the Pilgrims' fall harvest was very successful and plentiful. There was corn, fruits, and vegetables of all kinds, fish and meat that had been packed in salt or smoke cured over fires. They had enough food put away in stores to last through the coming winter. The pilgrims had beaten the odds. They built homes in the wilderness, they raised enough crops to keep themselves alive, and they were at peace with their neighbors. **Governor William Bradford,** proclaimed a day of thanksgiving that was to be shared by all of the people in the colony, including their neighboring Native American Indians.

The celebration of an annual gathering held following the harvest time went on for years. During the **American Revolution, circa** 1770, a day of national thanksgiving was suggested by the Continental Congress.

In **1863,** President Abraham Lincoln proclaimed a national day of thanksgiving, and since that time each President has issued a Thanksgiving proclamation, usually designating the fourth Thursday of November as the special holiday.

Thanksgiving is a time to thank God for all of the good things that he has bestowed upon us--the love and care of family members and friends; a healthy life, a successful career, a loving wife, caring children, and so many more blessing that we have received.

But what happens when happiness is difficult to muster; when there is very little food; when there is an empty seat at the table; when hope is hard to come by? When the foundation for our thankfulness is found in what we do not have, can we still find joy? In the midst of uncertain and tragic times we often find ourselves at a crossroads for our faith. We usually question God's wisdom, His power, and even His goodness. The outcome of our questions either strengthen our faith or leave it weakened by our seeming inability to trust a God we cannot pack neatly into our preconceived ideas.

When we root our joy in the unchanging and sovereign person of God, our faith is on an unmovable foundation and we live in a spirit of joy and thankfulness, in all circumstances.

God is the center of our salvation, not humankind. He is beyond comprehension but not beyond relationship. He is patient and gracious with us, but He does not bend our will. God is sovereign, wise, just, loving, holy, and infinitely indescribable. Our faith in Him is not based on our ability to understand the way he works. Our faith is based on Him, and he does not disappoint. He is God, and we submit to Him as we thank Him for all that we receive through His bounty.

Give thanks for that which we receive through Him.

DAY OF ASHURA

Islam is one of the three faiths that grew from Abraham, first known as Abram, who was God's chosen person to become the progenitor of the people of Israel and the founder of Judaism. They also include Christianity, and Islam.

Islam's origin began in the 7th century by Muhammad who claimed that the angel Gabriel visited him. During the angelic visits, which continued for 23 years until Muhammad's death, the angel purportedly revealed the words of Allah, (the Arabic word for "God" used by Muslims).

There are many sub-groups within Islam, the three major groups include Shia (Shiite), Sunni, and Sufi Muslims. Each practice Islam somewhat differently, yet all hold to the Qur'an as its holy book, the five pillars of Islam and the six doctrines of Islam.

The pillars include:

1. The testimony of faith (*Shahabad*): One god, Allah.
2. Prayer (*salat*): Five ritual prayers, performed each day.
3. Giving (*zakat*): Given once each year, (2.5 percent of income).
4. Fasting (sawin): Must not eat or drink from dawn to dusk during Ramadan.
5. Pilgrimage (*hajj*): Go to Mecca in Saudi Arabia at least once their lives.

The Key Doctrine of Islam include:

1. Belief in Allah as the one, creator, eternal and sovereign.
2. Belief in angels, both good and bad.
3. Belief in prophets: Include biblical prophets but end with Muhammad, Allah's prophet. (Jesus is considered one of the many prophets.)
4. Belief in the revelations of Allah, including some bible Scriptures in the Gospels and the Torah. The Qur'an is considered their holy book.
5. Belief in the Day of Judgment and an afterlife
6. Belief in predestination; Muslims believe that Allah has decreed everything that will happen.in his name

The Day of Ashura is principally celebrated by the Sunni Muslims, who refer to it as The Day of Atonement., as the day on which the Israelites were freed from the Pharaoh of Egypt. Whereas, the Shi'a Muslims commemorate The Day of Ashura as a day of protest against tyrant rulers especially the one who martyred Husayn Ali, the grandson of Muhammad, the third Imam, who was the apparent successor to Muhammad. Husayn was murdered, along with members of his family at the Battle of Karbala in 680 AD.

Sunni Muslims make up the largest number of members in Islam with about ninety percent counting its heritage. However, there are many other groups coming from countries, including Azerbaijan, Bahrain, Iran, Syria and Iraq.

Jesus is considered a prophet in the Qur'an, but not divine nor God's son. Many Muslims believe that Jesus was not crucified on a cross Jesus is not considered a Messiah or, "The way, the truth, and the life." John 14:6.

Salvation and eternal life in the Islam belief is based on good works, primary obedience to the five pillars, along with the other Qur'an teaching. This is much different than salvation as presented in the Bible. Salvation is based on God's grace through faith in Jesus Christ not on good works. Further, the Bible teaches the only way to spend eternity with God is through Jesus, not other gods.

THE ADVENT CALENDAR

The word **Advent** has a Latin origin....meaning *"the coming."* Or perhaps more accurately, *"coming toward."* For Christians, one of the greatest events of the year is the celebration of the birth of our Savior Jesus Christ. We acknowledge this as the greatest gift ever given by God to mankind. Jesus, the son of God, born into this world in human form and coming to live among us to show us the true nature of God, experiencing human joy and sorrow, and finally willing to go to the cross to die for us and pay for all human sins, so that we might have hope of life eternal.

The importance of this event caused many Christians to feel that having only **one day, Christmas,** wasn't enough for celebrating this incredible gift from God. Believers had such a sense of awe and overwhelming gratitude for what had happened that first **Christmas Day,** they felt a need for a period of preparation immediately beforehand. That way, they could take time to meditate on it, and also teach their children the tremendous significance of Christmas.

At first, the days preceding Christmas were marked off from December 1 with chalk on believers' doors. Then, in Germany in the late 19th century, the mother of a child named Gerhard Lang made her son an **Advent Calendar** comprised of 24 tiny sweets stuck on a cardboard. It reminded her son that the greatest celebration of the whole year was approaching. Anticipate it and be grateful.

When Gerhard grew up he went into the printing business and in 1908 he produced what is thought to be the first ever **Advent Calendar,** with small colored pictures for each day in Advent. Later on, he hit on an idea of making the pictures into little shuttered windows for each child to open day by day to heighten their sense of expectation of the coming of Christmas.

The idea of the Advent Calendar caught on and as the demand increased many versions were produced, some had Bible verses pertaining to the Advent period. Unfortunately, the custom came to an end with the beginning of World War I when cardboard was rationed and only allowed to be used for necessary projects. However,

In 1946, when rationing began to ease following the end of the Second World War, the tradition once again introduced the colorful little Advent Calendar. It was an instant success.

Sadly today, the Advent Calendar, still enormously popular with children, has lost its true meaning. Many children and their parents have no idea of the history of the little calendar or its true purpose, which is to prepare us for the celebration of the advent of the **Christ-child.** Even if they do know, most don't care. The makers of today's Advent Calendars are anxious only to sell their product, and many don't know or don't care about the meaning and the purpose of **Advent.** The calendars depict Santa Claus and his reindeer, snowmen, holly, mistletoe and all the secular trappings of Christmas, behind the little windows, often along with a piece of chocolate or some candy treat.

Fortunately however, Christian printers are still with us who manufacture calendars for children that unfold the story of the nativity with each window that is opened. We **Christian believers** pray that one day the whole world will be aware of the incredible wonder of the true meaning of **Advent** and Christmas.

Too often we under estimate the power of a touch, a radiance of a smile, or the sound of a kind word, a listening ear, an honest compliment, or the smallest act of caring. **Advent** may help you to remember that we **can** make it a **Christmas Day**, any day for those who come into our life.

"And we know that in all things God works for the good of those who love Him, who have been called according to His purpose" Romans 8:3

LET IT SNOW

In Genesis, Chapter 1, verses 3-4 it says, *"God said let there be light, and there was light. And the light was good."* And I said, let there be snow, and the snow was light, and the people rejoiced.

Winter is here. Officially, it began on December 21, as described by the Farmer's Almanac. The Almanac enjoys a remarkable record in weather projections with an 80% accuracy. It is often more correct than the National Meteorological Service. The editors of the Almanac base their predictions on three scientific disciplines in order to make their long-range forecasts: Solar science, the study of sunspots and solar activity; Climatology, the study of prevailing weather patterns; and Meteorology, the study of the atmospheric conditions.

Their outlook for weather conditions is based on temperature and precipitation deviations from averages, or norms, from a 30 year statistical data bank. This information is made available by the US Meteorological Agencies and is updated every 10 years. With all the scientific sophistication they still admit that nothing in the universe happens haphazardly, there is a cause and effect pattern to all phenomena.

So the Almanac predicts this winter's weather for New England; to be much colder than normal with near normal precipitation and below normal snowfall. The rainy periods will be in mid to late December with the coldest periods to be in late December through early to mid-January. The cold will return in mid-February and remain through the month. The snowiest periods will be in late

December and early to mid-March. The good news is spring begins the 20th of March, only fifteen days before Easter.

It seems that everybody talks about the weather but no one does anything about it. Mom use to say, "Put on your galoshes it looks like rain." But she couldn't start Or stop the rain from coming.

In Biblical times we had weather watchers. They weren't meteorologists but they knew about the weather conditions. In the Bible we read the following:

"The Pharisees and the Sadducees came, and to test him they asked him to show them a sign from Heaven. He answered them, 'When it is evening you say it will be fair weather, for the sky is red. And in the morning, it will be stormy today, for the sky is red and threatening. You know how to interrupt the appearance of the sky, but you can't interrupt the signs of the times." Math. 16: 1-2. NIV

We have given credit to sailors for having said, "Red sky in the morning, sailors take warning. Red sky at night, sailor's delight." It is scriptural.

"My little snowman Herman may serve to illustrate the point. In the winter some of our most popular activities are skating on the ponds, sliding down the slopes, skiing or just making angels in the snow. The angels have been sent to tell us of the birth of Jesus Christ. When the snow comes it is time to make a snowman. He tells us even more:

Let It Snow

We see the snowflakes falling as the winter storm begins,
Each flake tells us a story of God's forgiveness for our sins.
When the snow is deep and drifting, we can roll it in a ball,
 It's time to build a snowman, the greatest of them all.
 With all our work and effort, our labor and our strife,

We recall the promise of everlasting life.
The snowman has a carrot nose, a smile upon his face.
It's there to give God credit for life and saving grace.
The snowman has black charcoal eyes to keep a watchful view,
To remind us to look out for others, to help them if we choose.
God makes it very clear to us its part of the master plan, we must
Help others when and if we can.
The scarf around the snowman's neck is there to keep him warm,
The scarf is to remind us God's love is a guard from all harm.
The mitten cap upon his head is stunning, a colorful display,
It tells us that God rejoices when we stop and pray.
The outstretched arms of the snowman are open to receive.
Like the arms of God are always open, if only we believe.

RECIPE FOR CHRISTMAS JOY

Christmas. Everyone has a favorite recipe they like to use for special events. You may have one that is associated with Christmas and the holidays. Perhaps what needs to be done is to define **Christmas** and talk about its meaning. What then is Christmas, and why and how do we celebrate it? I want to share with you some thoughts about Christmas.

I turned to my **Bible,** in its concordance, and looked up the word **CHRISTMAS. It wasn't there.** I quickly went to my **Bible Dictionary** and found the definition. Christmas. It is the **anniversary of the birth of Jesus Christ.** Christmas is celebrated by most Protestant and Catholic believers on the **25th of December each year.** Eastern Orthodox churches celebrate Christmas on January 6th, and Armenian Churches on January 19th.The first mention of Christmas observances on December 25th was in the time of Constantine, about 325 AD. The actual date of the birth of Christ is not known. The word **CHRISTMAS** is formed by the name of **Christ+ Mass,** meaning a mass or religious service in commemoration of Jesus' birth.

We find ourselves preparing for a celebration of the **Birth of God's Son..** The Christian Church seasons of **Advent** and **Christmas** are rich with traditions and symbolism. Many of which had their origins in pagan traditions. So Christians included many of these events in spiritual ways to help themselves, as well as new believers, to focus on **Jesus Christ.**

One **event** that is as very popular is the celebration of **Advent.** The word ADVENT means **"the coming or arrival."** In pre-Christian Germany and Scandinavia people gathered to celebrate the return of the sun after the winter solstice. That is a time when the sun reaches its highest or lowest point in the sky. A circular wreath made of evergreens with candles placed on it represented the circle of the year and the life that endured throughout the winter. As the days grew longer the people lit the candles to offer thanks to the **Sun God** for the light.

Lutherans in eastern Germany started the custom of the **Advent Wreath** as a Christian act of worship. Today we celebrate **Advent** with the wreath and the progressive lighting of candles. A circular wreath of evergreen boughs is made and a candle is lit each Sunday for four weeks before Christmas.

The first candle in the wreath is the **HOPE Candle.** It is usually purple, depicting that Jesus is the light of the world and turns the darkness of the world to light.

The second candle is the **Bethlehem Candle,** a blue candle. It is also called the **LOVE candle. God** loves us even more than we can possibly comprehend, He wants us to love one another.

The third candle is the **Shepherd's Candle,** pink or rose in color, typifies the act of sharing Christ. God sent his only Son to the world not to punish or condemn the world but to have our sins forgiven by our belief in Jesus. It is called the **JOY Candle.**

The fourth candle is the **Angel's Candle.** It is the candle of love and tells of the final coming of the Christ. It is also known as the **PEACE candle**. It is colored red. God wants all mankind to live in a peaceful world.

The largest candle, color white, is placed in the center of the wreath. It is the **CHRIST Candle.** It is traditionally lit on Christmas Eve.

The word **Advent** means **"coming or arrival."** The focus of the entire season is the celebration of the birth of Jesus Christ and the anticipation of the return of **Christ the King** at his second coming. The white candle is always lighted on Christmas Eve.

CHRISTMAS TREES are another familiar symbol of Christmas. At this time of year, when the leaves of other trees have turned brown and fallen to the ground, the evergreen tree keep its fresh green look, encouraging us to be thankful for our lives. It is the symbol of **LIFE.**

By the beginning of the 19th century all of Germany had adopted the use of the green fir tree as the **Christmas tree.** They decorated the tree with candles and stars, hand-made ornaments, tiny toys and gilded nuts, so all could enjoy the time of Jesus' birth. The custom of the Christmas tree was brought to the United States by the Pennsylvania Germans in the 1820's. In 1923 President Calvin Coolidge held the first lighting of an outdoor tree at the White House, thereby starting a long-standing tradition. President Obama, his family and guests, lit the White House tree on Friday December 6 at 4:30 PM, in the traditional Christmas ceremony. The tree is a 40 foot, live Colorado Spruce decorated with more than 3,000 lights.

To Christians, the lighted tree, with candles or electric lights, and the Advent wreathes reminds us that **Jesus is the Light for the world, the light that we should follow.** Scripture reminds us:

Jesus said: *"I am the light for the world. Follow me, and You won't be walking in the dark. You will have*

There are many traditions and symbols of Christmas. They include the Advent Wreath, the Advent Calendar, The Christmas Tree, Christmas Carols, Christmas Bells, Nativity scenes, Snowmen, Poinsettia plants, Fruit Cakes, Christmas greeting cards, mistletoe and Yule logs. And we could go on and on. But one traditional favor is having a special recipe for Christmas, and here it is:

Christmas Joy

Ingredients: 1/2 cup of **HUGS**
4 cups of LOVE
4 teaspoons of **KISSES**
1 cup of holiday **CHEER**
3 teaspoons of **CHRISTMAS SPIRITS**
1/2 cup of **PEACE on EARTH**
2 cups of "**GOODWLL TOWARDS MAN**"
1 sprig of **MISTLETOE**
A medium sized bag of **SNOW FLAKES**

Preparation:
Mix hugs, kisses, and love until consistent. Blend in holiday cheer,
peace on earth, Christmas spirits and goodwill towards man.
Use the mixture to fill a large warm heart,
where it can be stored for a life time.
It will never go bad.

Serve as desired under mistletoe, sprinkled generously with special Christmas snowflakes.

Christmas Joy is especially good when served when singing carols at family get-togethers. This recipe provides numerous servings for **one and all.**

To earn God's favor, Christians are to live a life of obedience to Jesus Christ and to the teachings of all scripture, both Old and New Testament. Christians are to be strong and compliant in their **Faith.**

Paul's letter to the Galatians explains:

"Is the law therefore opposed to the promises of God?

Absolutely not! For if a law had been given that could
Impart life, then righteousness would have certainly come
By the law. But scripture declares that the whole world
Is a prisoner of sin, so that what was promised, being given
Through the faith in Jesus Christ, might be given to whose
Who believe?
Before this faith came, we were held prisoners by the law.
Locked up until faith should be revealed. So the law was put
In charge to lead us to Christ, that we might be justified by
Faith. Now that Faith has come we are no longer under the
Law. Galatians 3: 21-23

Simply said: **What does the Lord require of us?**

a. **To act justly,**
b. **Love mercy,**
c. **Have faith in Jesus Christ,**
d. **Walk humbly with God.**

Pastor Murray Hunt, preaching a short sermon to a church he was leaving once said,

"Love the Lord, and do as you please."

THE SIGNIFICANCE OF CHRISTMAS

Scripture: *"Let the heavens be glad, and let the earth rejoice before the Lord, for God is coming to judge the earth. God will judge the righteousness, and the peoples in his truth."* **Psalm 96: 11, 13b**

Every time you look at a calendar or refer to a day, or write down a date you are using **Jesus Christ** as a reference point. The history of Jesus is divided into two parts **BC** (*before Christ*) and **AD** (*anno Domini, in the year of the Lord*). Every other event in history and every event recorded on our calendars today is dated by how many days and years it has been since **Jesus** appeared on earth.

Even our birthday is dated by *His birthday*. Then why shouldn't we celebrate His birthday?

Scripture proclaims that God is coming, He sent his son Jesus, in His place not to judge the world,

But to save us from our sins.

When the angels announced the birth of Jesus to the shepherds keeping watch over their flocks near Bethlehem, the first Christmas night, they were promised that it would *"bring great joy, for all the people.'* For how many people? For **all of the people**.

For some, getting ready for Christmas seems like more of a hassle than a time of happiness. For many it becomes a source of stress and frustration. They feel pressure, not pleasure. It's a duty not a delight. They **endure** Christmas rather than enjoy it.

There are many possible reasons that may make us feel uneasy. Lonely or even depressed. We may dread spending time with oddball relatives. Maybe relationships are strained and uncomfortable in our family. Maybe we don't have anyone to be with this Christmas. Maybe we are confined and can't get out. Christmas may remind you of all of your losses or hurts or how things have changed. You may have a religious background that doesn't include Christmas, or you may have no faith at all. Watching others celebrate may make you feel uneasy. Maybe you are just exhausted and worn out from all that has happened to your life this past year.

This Christmas believe that God cares deeply about how you feel. Regardless of your background, religion, problems or circumstances.

Christmas really is the best news you could get. Beneath all of the visible signs and sounds of Christmas there are some simple yet profound truths that can transform your life for the better here on earth, to the forever in eternity. There is nothing more important for you to understand than the implications of Christmas in your life.

When we pause and consider the significance of Christmas we can receive and enjoy the best and most wonderful gift ever given. **It is God's Christmas gift to you.**

God's Christmas gift has three qualities that make it unique:

> First, it is the **most expensive gift** you will ever receive. It is Priceless. **Jesus** paid for it with His life.

> Second, it is the only gift that you will receive that will **last forever.** Christianity is **eternal.**

> Finally, it is **an extremely practical gift**—one you will use every day

> For the rest of your life and you won't have to exchange it for color or size.

On the first Christmas night, the angels announced three purposes for the birth of Jesus Christ:

Christmas is a time for celebration!
Christmas is a time for salvation.
Christmas is a time for reconciliation.

THE CHRISTMAS STORY

Luke 2: 1-20 NIV

And it came to pass in those days, that there went out a decree from Caesar Augustus, that all the world should be taxed. And this taxing was first made when Cyrenius was governor of Syria.

And all went to be taxed, every one into his own city. And Joseph also went up from Galilee, out of the city of Nazareth, into Judaea, unto the city of David, which is called Bethlehem; (because he was of the house and lineage of David) To be taxed with Mary his exposed wife, being great with child.

And so it was, that, while they were there, the days were accomplished that she should be delivered. And she brought forth her firstborn son, and wrapped him in swaddling clothes, and laid him in a manger; because there was no room for them in the inn.

And there were in the same country shepherds abiding in the field, keeping watch over their flock my night. And lo, the angel of the Lord came upon them and the glory of the Lord shone round about them: and they were sore afraid.

And the angel said unto them, Fear not: for behold I bring you good tiding of great joy, which shall be to all people. For unto you is born this day in the city of David a Savior, which is Christ the Lord. And this shall be a sign unto you; ye shall find the babe wrapped in swaddling clothes, lying in a manger.

And suddenly there was with the angel a multitude of the heavenly host praising God and saying, Glory to God in the highest and on earth peace, good will toward men.

And it came to pass, as the angels were gone away from them into heaven, the shepherds said one to another, Let us now go even unto

Bethlehem and see this thing which is come to pass, which the Lord hath made known unto us. And they came with haste, and found Mary and Joseph and the babe lying in a manger.

And when they had seen it, they made known abroad the saying which was told them concerning the child. And all they that heard it wondered at those things which were told them by the shepherds. But Mary kept all these things, and pondered them in her heart.

And the shepherds returned, glorifying and praising God for all the things that they had heard and seen, as it was told unto them."

Amen

MAKE A NEW YEAR'S RESOLUTION

The practice of making New Year's resolutions goes back over 3,000 years to the ancient Babylonians. There is something about the start of a new year that gives us the feeling of a fresh start and a new beginning. In reality, there is no difference between December 31 and January first. Nothing mystical occurs at midnight on New Year's Eve. The Bible does not speak for or against the concept of New Year's resolutions. However, if a Christian determines to make a New Year's resolution, what kind of resolution should he or she make?

Common New Year's resolutions are commitments to quit smoking, to stop drinking, to manage money more wisely, and to spend more time with members of your family. By far, the most common resolution is to lose weight in connection with exercising and to eat more healthful food. These are all good goals to set. But, 1 Timothy 4:8 tells us to exercise in perspective: "For physical training is of some value, but godliness has value for all things, holding promise for both the present life and the life to come." The vast majority of resolutions, even among Christians, are in relation to physical things and this should not be their limit.

Many Christians make New Year's resolutions to pray more, to read the Bible every day, and to attend church more regularly. These are excellent goals. However, these resolutions often fail, just like the non-spiritual resolutions, because there is no power in a New Year's a resolution. Resolving to start or stop dong a certain activity has no value unless you have the proper motivation for stopping or starting that activity. For example. Why do you want to read the Bible every day? Is it to honor God and grow spiritually, or is it because you have heard it a good thing to do? Why do you want to lose weight? Is it to honor God with your body, or is it for vanity, to honor yourself?

Philippians 4:13 tells us, "I can do everything through Him who gives me strength. "John 15; 5 declares, "I am the vine, you are the branches. If a man remains in me and I in Him he will bear much fruit; apart from me you can do nothing." If God is the center of your New Year's resolution, it has a good chance for success, depending on your commitment to it. If it is God' will for something to be fulfilled, He will enable you to fulfill it. If it is a resolution not honoring God and not agreement in God's Word, we will not receive God's help in fulfilling it.

So, what sort of resolutions should a Christian make? Here are some suggestions:

- Pray to the Lord for wisdom in regards to what resolutions to make.
- Pray for wisdom as to how to fulfill the goals that He gives you.
- Rely on God's strength to help you
- Find an accountability partner who will help you and encourage you.
- Don't become discouraged with occasional failures, instead allow them to strengthen your resolve.
- Don't become proud or vain, but give God the glory.
- Psalm 37:5-6 says, *"Commit your way to the Lord, trust him and he will do this: He will make your righteousness shine like the dawn, the justice of your cause like the noonday sun."*

NEW YEAR'S PRAYER

Dear Father:
Another year has come and gone,
Its days went all too fast.
Did I purse eternal things?
Those values that will last?
Surround me with its care,
And seldom heard your gentle voice
Speak softly to my ear?

When I review this year and see
Those things that might have been,
I ask you with a humble heart
For time to try again.
Forgive me for my failures, Lord,
And bless each coming day.
I thank you for a second chance.
In Jesus name I pray.

Amen

AMEN

Amen is a Hebrew word commonly explained to mean, "So Be It." It expresses agreement and signifies the truth. Saying or using Amen means that all is well, and all that has preceded it in prayer, song or verse is true, trustworthy and reliable.

Amen is used by Christians, Jews, and Muslims and has become an integral part of the worship service. It concludes hymns, prayers, creeds and declarations.

In the Koran, the Muslim Bible, the first Surah is recited using the word Amen.

The word Amen is found thirteen times in the Hebrew Bible. In the New Testament it is used 119 times. Whenever Jesus wished to emphasize the importance of what he said he prefaced his words with it.

In keeping with the religious themes and traditions of this book, "Tomorrow's Sights and Sounds," we feel it is proper to conclude with an Amen! AMEN!

Printed in the United States
By Bookmasters